# HUME'S
# RELIGIOUS
# NATURALISM

Lou Reich

University Press of America,® Inc.
Lanham • New York • Oxford

Copyright © 1998 by
**University Press of America,® Inc.**
4720 Boston Way
Lanham, Maryland 20706

12 Hid's Copse Rd.
Cummor Hill, Oxford OX2 9JJ

All rights reserved
Printed in the United States of America
British Library Cataloging in Publication Information Available

**Library of Congress Cataloging-in-Publication Data**

Reich, Lou.
Hume's religious naturalism / Lou Reich.
p. cm.
Includes bibliographical references and index.
1. Hume, David, 1711-1776—Religion. 2. Naturalism—Religious aspects—History of doctrines—18th century. I. Title.
B1499.R45R45 1997 210'.92 —DC21 97-38956 CIP

ISBN 0-7618-0981-3 (cloth: alk. ppr.)
ISBN 0-7618-0982-1 (pbk: alk. ppr.)

∞™ The paper used in this publication meets the minimum requirements of American National Standard for information Sciences—Permanence of Paper for Printed Library Materials, ANSI Z39.48—1984

# Contents

| | |
|---|---|
| Preface | v |
| Introduction | vii |
| Chapter I<br>Religion and "Natural Belief" in Hume's *Dialogues*<br>Notes | 1<br>24 |
| Chapter II<br>"Strong" vs. "Weak" Natural Belief and *Dialogue* XII<br>Notes | 29<br>44 |
| Chapter III<br>Supernaturalism vs. "Religious Naturalism"<br>Notes | 47<br>69 |
| Chapter IV<br>"Religious Naturalism" and Miracles<br>Notes | 73<br>96 |
| Summary and Conclusions | 103 |
| Bibliography | 109 |
| Index | 113 |

# Preface

It is a sad irony that the severe impoverishment of philosophy in mid-twentieth century analytic thought was undertaken ostensibly on the basis of the philosophy of David Hume. His metaphysical concerns were construed purely negatively. The way in which his epistemological skepticism was mitigated by a robust naturalism was barely understood. His ethical concerns tended to be relegated to the realm of nonsense. And his aesthetic views and sensibilities were rarely if ever appreciated at all.

This work presents a conception of Hume's overall philosophical stance which is derived from a focus on his *Dialogues Concerning Natural Religion* and *The Natural History of Religion*. A broad context is provided by frequent references to *A Treatise Of Human Nature* and to *An Enquiry Concerning Human Understanding* as well as to other relevant essays and letters written by Hume.

Religious Naturalism is a complex tapestry woven of aesthetic, ethical, epistemological and metaphysical elements. The religious element in Hume's writings, which some commentators see as a transcendentalist position, is interpreted as an immanentist religiosity akin to that of Spinoza and Einstein.

Hume's three "strong natural beliefs" in "self," objects and causality, come together as a metaphysical faith in the ultimate reality of a shared cosmos. Hume's aesthetic response is expressed as a sense of the sublimity of the cosmos even in the midst of skeptical doubt. In Hume's religious naturalism his epistemological skepticism casts doubt on and tempers his metaphysical faith. It is shown that Hume's overriding ethical concern was to further the happiness of humanity by replacing the "pernicious superstition" of supernaturalism with an immanentist position which affirms the inexplicable presence of an eternal cosmos. This position is what is here termed Religious Naturalism.

I am deeply indebted to Professor Oliver A. Johnson, whose graduate seminars on David Hume's *Treatise* and on Hume's views on Religion and Ethics provided the initial impetus for a dissertation which resulted in the present work. For Professor Johnson's guidance on a Proposition which I submitted on David Hume, and his many helpful comments on the present manuscript, I am greatly appreciative.

I would like to thank Professor John Martin Fischer, for his continuing encouragement and the detailed suggestions and comments he provided throughout the course of my writing the present work.

I would also like to thank Professor Alexander Rosenberg for his encouragement during informal discussions of the manuscript.

I am grateful to Doctor Frank Verges for reading the manuscript and providing suggestions for the final draft.

The extent of my appreciation for Doctor Shari Neller Starrett's input during numerous discussions concerning the overall project of this work cannot be adequately expressed.

Portions of Chapter III, "Supernaturalism vs. Religious Naturalism," were presented at the 24th annual Hume Society Conference held at Monterey, California, in the summer of 1997, as a paper titled "Hume's Religious Naturalism." I am happy that Stanley Tweyman consented to comment on the paper and I am grateful for his kind permission to cite his book, *Scepticism And Natural Belief in Hume's Dialogues Concerning Natural Religion*.

My thanks to J.C.A. Gaskin for permission to quote from his book, *Hume's Philosophy of Religion*. And thanks to Nettie DeBill at Stanford University Press for securing permission to quote from H.E. Root's edition of Hume's *Natural History of Religion*.

Finally, a special note of thanks is due to Rae Reich for typing, proofreading, editing, indexing, comments, and for her "argumentativeness," which proved to be invaluable.

# Introduction

This work argues for an interpretation of David Hume as a "religious naturalist." This is a view of Hume made plausible by a consideration of Hume's various writings on religion. It is seen that in these writings Hume opposed his own faith to supernaturalistic faith. At stake, for Hume, was the greater happiness of humanity.

A number of commentators have detected a religious belief in Hume's writing. I differ with these commentators in my interpretation of that religious belief. While Tweyman, Pike and others see it as a transcendental faith, I see it as an immanentist one.

Hume's "religious naturalism" is Hume's attribution of order or design to "nature," where "nature" is seen as a shared cosmos whose immanent origin of order is secret and inexplicable. It is this shared cosmos which, for Hume, is the ultimate reality. Hume's skepticism is not denied, but rather it is likened to the doubt which often attends supernaturalistic faith. Just as faith and doubt are related in supernaturalism, skepticism concerning his own metaphysical position is an element of Hume's "religious naturalism."

# Chapter I

# Religion and "Natural Belief" in Hume's *Dialogues*

Nothing in Hume's other works quite prepares the reader of his *Dialogues Concerning Natural Religion* for the apparent shift of position that one of its characters (Philo) makes at its end. For it appears that Philo, who has substantially undermined the argument for God's existence from the "design" of the universe, has made certain concessions to religion at the end of the *Dialogues* (Part XII) that ill accord with the whole tenor of his position throughout the preceding parts of the work.

Throughout the preceding parts of the *Dialogues* Philo had been arguing, against Cleanthes, a philosophical theologian, that the existence of an "intelligent designer" of the universe cannot be demonstrated. Cleanthes had put forth the argument that (roughly) there is a design or an order in the "works of nature," and that this design or order bears sufficient analogy to the works of "human art and contrivance" for "just rules" of analogical reasoning to license the inference that the design in nature has an "intelligent designer" as its cause, just as the design in "human art and contrivance" is derived from an intelligent cause.

This a posteriori argument for God's existence provides the main focus of discussion in the *Dialogues*. And, as has been said, Cleanthes' version of the "design argument" is substantially undermined by Philo. But both Philo and Cleanthes together object to an a priori argument for God's existence given by the third character in the *Dialogues,* i.e., Demea, a dogmatic thinker who has neither the "accurate philosophical turn" of Cleanthes, nor the facility for argumentation that Philo has.

As far as the *arguments* in the *Dialogues* are concerned it seems clear that Hume's intention is to show that both the a posteriori and the a priori versions of the theistic arguments for God's existence are unsound. But it is this fact which gives rise to a continuing controversy over the proper interpretation of the concessions Philo appears to make in Part XII.

Philo's arguments against Cleanthes throughout the *Dialogues* are based on Humean doctrines. They are based on his doctrine of "impressions and ideas," according to which ideas arise only from impressions; these "perceptions" are the only proper objects of human understanding; and causal inferences may be made only when we have observed the putative cause and the putative effect to be constantly conjoined, spatially contiguous, and to have the same order of temporal priority in all observed cases. Furthermore, when we infer from an effect to a cause we cannot return from the cause to infer still other effects. Nor can we posit more in the cause than is sufficient to produce the effect. But if Philo's arguments are Humean, how are we to understand Hume's actual position when Philo says that, "no one...pays more profound adoration to the Divine Being" than himself?[1] What is Philo's meaning, and what bearing does it have on Hume's views when he says "a person, seasoned with a just sense of the imperfections of natural reason, will fly to revealed truth with the greatest avidity...?"[2] Statements like these are not called for by the argument. What is their import?

I make no pretense to be able to put an end to the controversies in the present work. A number of questions arise in the endeavor to understand the significance of Hume's *Dialogues,* some of which are the following: Is it Philo who represents Hume, as Norman Kemp Smith believes?[3] Is it Cleanthes, since Hume says that he makes Cleanthes the "hero?"[4] Perhaps there is an "implicit argument" in the *Dialogues,* and all the "explicit characters" contribute to it, as Hurlbutt argues.[5] Is Philo being ironic, or does he mean (in a literal sense) what he says?

Is the belief in an "intelligent designer of the world" a "natural belief" for Hume? A number of commentators take the view that it is. An affirmative answer to this question, it could be maintained, would go a long way toward clearing up the puzzling ending of the *Dialogues.* It could be argued that while Hume does not think that the teleological argument establishes the existence of God, he also does not think the severe criticisms that can be directed at the argument can succeed in dislodging a positive attitude toward the argument's conclusion. It could then be argued that this fact helps to explain Philo's prima facie affirmation of God's existence in Part XII.

The above question is a much disputed one, not a few commentators having joined the fray. Stanley Tweyman gives an analysis of Humean "natural beliefs," arguing that the belief in an "intelligent designer" has the same status in the *Dialogues* that causation, the existence of an objective world, and the belief in personal identity have in Hume's other works.[6]

Hurlbutt, Prado, and Harris each agree with this position, in general.[7] Norman Kemp Smith, P.S. Wadia, and B.A.O. Williams are among those who disagree with Tweyman's view.[8]

I will discuss Tweyman's analysis of Humean "natural beliefs" at length, and I will discuss Hurlbutt's similar though somewhat different approach to the conclusion that the belief in an "intelligent designer" is a natural one for Hume.

I believe that the treatment of this position by Tweyman and Hurlbutt provides the strongest arguments for adding the belief in an "intelligent designer" to the list of Humean "natural beliefs." However, my own view is that these arguments fail to establish what they intend.

I will argue that Tweyman's analysis of Humean "natural beliefs," (1) incorrectly interprets certain conditions of natural beliefs that he (Tweyman) includes in his list of conditions, and (2) that Tweyman's list of conditions for a "natural belief" is incomplete, i.e., it does not include certain "facts" related to "natural beliefs" that Hume himself was keen to emphasize, and (3) that Hume himself comes very close (at least) to explicitly denying that belief in an "intelligent designer" is a natural belief. My discussion of (1), (2) and (3) will receive textual support from Hume's *Enquiry Concerning Human Understanding, A Treatise of Human Nature,* and *The Natural History of Religion.* I will argue that the conclusions reached undermine Hurlbutt's analysis as well as Tweyman's.

The bulk of Tweyman's argument lies in his construal of Part XII of the *Dialogues,* together with an independent analysis of Hume's treatment of causality, objective existence and personal identity, as natural beliefs.[9]

Hurlbutt argues that Cleanthes' "illustrative analogies" in Part III indicate that the belief in an "intelligent designer" is being treated as a "natural" one.[10] I think he makes a good case for this view with regard to Cleanthes' position. Tweyman also has recourse to these analogies as well as to other Parts of the *Dialogues.* Tweyman argues that Philo's remarks in Part XII help "to bring him in line with Cleanthes' position in Part III."[11] This is crucial. As I see it, Philo and Cleanthes must be shown to agree on the point that belief in an intelligent design is natural. Then the view that Hume holds that belief in an "intelligent designer" is a natural belief could be considered a plausible view. It must also be shown, at the very least, that this view is not inconsistent with the positions Hume takes in his own person in his other works. On this latter point, Tweyman says,

> The position I will defend is that the belief in an intelligent designer of the world satisfies all the criteria of a natural belief and therefore, must be regarded as being such a belief.[12]

I turn now to Stanley Tweyman's treatment of Humean natural beliefs, focusing on the "non-controversial cases" of such beliefs.[13] Tweyman correctly points out that a proper examination of "natural beliefs" in the *Dialogues* requires a preliminary examination of the "non-controversial cases," in Hume's other works.[14] He says, "...we must know the essential features of natural beliefs; and we must know what difference it makes whether or not a belief is a natural belief."[15]

Tweyman's analysis results in six criteria for Humean natural beliefs. I will list these criteria and then examine his documentation and argumentation for each one in turn. Tweyman's criteria for Humean "natural beliefs" are as follows:

> 1) A Belief Classified as a Natural Belief cannot be One Which can be Fully Analyzed in Terms of Hume's Account of Perceptions, or Impressions and Ideas.
> 2) Because a Natural Belief Goes Beyond the Data of Experience, the Awareness Accompanying a Natural Belief is Always a Substitute for the Putative Object of that Belief.
> 3) In the Case of a Natural Belief, We are Unable to Explicate the Putative Referent to the Belief.
> 4) What We Believe Naturally May not Be at All.
> 5) A Natural Belief is Unavoidable and Therefore Universal.
> 6) A Natural Belief is Always One Which is "an Affair of too Great Importance to be Trusted to Our Uncertain Reasonings and Speculations."[16]

In his treatment of criterion number (1), Tweyman begins by examining, "a case where the belief is fully analyzed in this way."[17] He quotes Hume as saying, "We cannot form to ourselves a just idea of the taste of a pineapple, without having actually tasted it."[18] This is a case where an impression of sensation causes us to have an idea. It is a case where the idea of the taste of pineapple is a "simple idea," and it is derived from a "simple impression," i.e., the experience of having tasted a pineapple. Hume says, "...every simple idea has a simple impression, which resembles it; and every simple impression a correspondent idea."[19] A belief, Hume says, "...may be most accurately defin'd (as), a lively idea related to or associated with a present impression."[20] In this sense then, the belief we have regarding the taste of a pineapple will be analyzed solely in terms of impressions and ideas. But this is not the case for "natural beliefs."[21]

Tweyman asks us to compare the case of belief just referred to with what he regards as one of the "non-controversial" cases of a "natural belief." This is the belief in personal identity.[22] He quotes a lengthy passage from Hume's *Treatise* where Hume is talking about the fact that some philosophers "imagine" that they are conscious of a self. The relevant part of the passage is this:

> It must be some one impression, that gives rise to every real idea. But self or person is not any one impression, but that to which our several impressions and ideas are supposed to have a reference. If any impression gives rise to the idea of self, that impression must continue invariably the same, thro' the whole course of our lives; since self is supposed to exist after that manner. But there is no impression that exists after that manner. Pain and pleasure, grief and joy, passions and sensations succeed each other, and never all exist at the same time. It cannot, therefore, be from any of these impressions, or from any other, that the idea of self is deriv'd; and consequently there is no such idea.[23]

Hume does seem to think that the belief in self or personal identity is a natural belief. His problem is in giving a satisfactory analysis of its genesis. After relating his "theater of perceptions" view of the "mind" he says, "There is properly no *simplicity* in it at any one time, nor *identity* in different; whatever natural propension we may have to imagine that simplicity and identity."[24] So, at least it can be argued that Hume held that the belief in a simple, identical self "may" result from a "natural propension" to "imagine" such.

Tweyman holds that in order for a belief to be fully analyzable in terms of impressions and ideas it must satisfy two conditions: (1) the belief must be derived entirely from the correspondent impression, and (2) the content of the belief must be the same as the impression which gave rise to it.[25] We can see that the belief in self or personal identity fails to satisfy either condition. In the passage quoted, Hume says what it would be like to have an impression of self and then says, "But there is no impression that exists after that manner," so condition (1) is not satisfied. (1) is not satisfied because (1) requires that a belief be derived from an impression, and the belief in personal identity is not so derived. The satisfaction of (1) is a necessary condition for the satisfaction of (2). So, if (1) is not satisfied, then (2) is not either.

The belief in the existence of an external world or the continued and independent existence of body also fails to satisfy these two conditions. As Tweyman points out, Hume holds that it is a "contradiction in terms" to think that the senses could provide us with an impression of the continued existence of body. For this would be to suppose that "...the senses continue to operate, even after they have ceas'd all manner of operations."[26] And the senses could not give us an impression of an independent existence, since this would be to suppose that they give us an impression of something distinct from the impression itself. But, as Hume points out, "they convey to us nothing but a single perception, and never give us the least intimation of anything beyond."[27] Nevertheless, we do naturally believe in an external world. Hume holds that we,

> must assent to the principle concerning the existence of the body...we may well ask, what causes us to believe in the existence of body? but 'tis vain to ask, Whether there be body or not? That is a point, which we must take for granted in all our reasonings.[28]

Nature has not left this to our choice.[29] So, with regard to the belief in the continuing and independent existence of body, the first condition for a belief to be fully analyzable in terms of impressions and ideas cannot be met. And since the first condition cannot be met, the second condition cannot be met either.[30]

Now, the belief in causality is also a natural belief. But Hume holds that this belief does arise from an impression. It is not an impression of sensation from which this belief arises, but rather, it is an impression of "reflexion."[31] Objects are never perceived to have a necessary connection between them. But on the observation that two objects are constantly conjoined, and that they are "contiguous" in time and space, having the same order of temporal priority, the mind forms a habit of inferring the one object whenever it observes the other. This habit is determined by custom. And it is the "impression" or "determination," Hume says, "which affords me the idea of necessity."[32]

Tweyman argues persuasively that on Hume's treatment of our belief in causality, it also fails to meet the two conditions which must be met in order for a belief to be fully analyzable in terms of impressions and ideas. He points out that the impression of reflection that enters into Hume's treatment, "...give us no insight whatever into the actual connection between objects."[33] This means that the belief in causal connections does not arise from an impression of those connections. We would have to have an impression of sensation whose content is "power," or "efficacy" or "necessity" (Hume regards these as "nearly synonimous"),[34] but we do not. Since the belief in causality between objects does not derive from an impression of causal connections between objects it fails to meet the first condition. Also, since we regard the connection to be in objects, the belief in causality is not confined to the habit generated in the mind. And so the belief is not exhausted in the content of the impression which gives rise to it. The foregoing analysis is designed to show that there is no case of a natural belief which can be fully analyzed in terms of Hume's account of impressions and ideas.

Tweyman's second criterion for a "natural belief" is, "Because a natural belief goes beyond the data of experience, the awareness accompanying a 'natural belief' is always a substitute for the putative object of that belief." With regard to causality the "awareness" we would need would be an awareness of "power" or "necessity" in objects. But we do not have the impression of sensation that would be required to give us such an "awareness." And, as Tweyman points out, we could not derive that awareness from intuition or deduction. In the case of the natural belief in causation we substitute the inner awareness, or impression of reflection, for an outer awareness of determination or necessity. But there is no such outer awareness. The reason we take the inner determination of habit to be a determination between external objects is our tendency towards psychological projection. Hume says, "...the mind has a great propensity to spread itself on external objects ...," and that is why, "...we suppose necessity and power to lie in the objects we consider, not in the mind, that considers them."[35]

Hume gives a similar analysis of our "natural belief" in the existence of an external world to the analysis he gives regarding causation. The difference here is that we do not project an inner impression onto objects, but rather, we simply "feign" the continued existence of objects. We suppose that objects continue independently of the mind, even though our perceptions are varied and fleeting. Our perceptions are interrupted, but, "we may remove the seeming interruption by feigning a continu'd being."[36] It is this feigned "continu'd being," made up out of whole cloth, that is taken to be an external object.[37] Tweyman says, correctly, that when Hume speaks of the activity of substitution involved in our natural beliefs he refers to it as "feigning."[38] It is "some lively impressions of memory" that give rise to our "propension" to feign the continued and independent existence of objects, and this same propensity "bestows a vivacity on that fiction," i.e., it makes us believe it.[39] In the case of personal identity, we attribute identity to perceptions, "because of the union of ideas in the imagination, when we reflect on them."[40] We then take the imagined identity to be real. In each case of a "natural belief," then, we take what is feigned, imagined, or projected to be the putative object of that belief. If we take the feigning, imagining, or projecting to be the "awareness" that accompanies a "natural belief," then we can say, with Tweyman, that "the awareness accompanying a natural belief is always a substitute for the putative object of that belief." This is a plausible account of Hume's treatment of such "substitution."

The third criterion proposed for a natural belief is, "In the case of a natural belief, we are unable to explicate the putative referent of the belief." With regard to this criterion Tweyman says that when we hold a particular natural belief we are not cognizant of precisely how we came to hold that belief, nor are we aware of what, precisely, is before the mind when we hold the belief, "nor of the alleged feature to which the natural belief supposedly has a reference."[41] So, we do not know what a causal connection between objects really is. We do not know how the self comes to have identity, and "we do not understand the nature of an object which possesses a continued and independent existence."[42]

The fourth criterion is, "What we naturally believe may not *be* at all." Since we have no direct experience of what we naturally believe, we cannot prove that what we believe obtains actually does obtain. We cannot prove that there are objects. We cannot prove that there are causal connections between objects. And, we cannot prove that there is personal identity, call it "proper identity." Objects, causal connections, and identity may not *be* at all. Tweyman says that, "...natural belief is unaffected by whatever is actually the case with respect to these (aforementioned) matters, given that our assent is not based on genuine insight."[43]

Tweyman's fifth criterion for a Humean "natural belief" is that, "A natural belief is unavoidable and therefore universal." In explaining this criterion Tweyman points out that in the section entitled "Of Scepticism with regard to the Senses," in the *Treatise,* Hume speaks of the skeptic continuing to reason and believe even though a defense of reason cannot be provided by reason. On the question of the existence of body, in the same section, Hume writes that the skeptic,

> must assent to the principle concerning the existence of body, tho' he cannot pretend by any argument of philosophy to maintain its veracity. Nature has not left this to his choice, and has doubtless esteem'd it an affair of too great importance to be trusted to our uncertain reasonings and speculations.[44]

The unavoidability of a natural belief is due to the fact that Nature has not left it to our choice whether to believe or not to believe.[45] Nature causes us to believe in body by way of a concurrence of "qualities of the imagination" with "certain qualities peculiar to some impressions."[46] Tweyman is interested in emphasizing the fact that Hume holds that there must be certain qualities present in our impressions in order for "Nature" to give rise to a natural belief. He says:

> In the case of the belief in body, the qualities the impressions must possess are constancy and coherence. For the belief in causality, the quality impressions

must possess is constant conjunction. The same type of analysis is what Hume sought to provide in the section on "Personal Identity." To speak of a natural belief as unavoidable, therefore, means that given certain perceptions with certain specifiable characteristics, the imagination will generate the awareness or belief in question—a belief which experience alone can never yield.[47]

Tweyman also points out that a "natural belief" is a "ready target" for the Pyrrhonian skeptic. He then refers the reader to that portion of the *Enquiry Concerning Human Understanding* where Hume talks about "action and employment, and the occupations of common life" as constituting a refutation of such an excessive skepticism.[48] He concludes this portion of his treatment of Humean "natural beliefs" by saying,

> We can see, therefore, that the unavoidability and universality of a given natural belief can be made manifest by showing the influence of instinct (Nature), and therefore, the impotence of skeptical arguments, in regard to this belief.[49]

The sixth criterion of a natural belief is that such a belief is of too great an importance for nature to trust to our reasoning. Tweyman sees this importance in two respects. The first respect is that it "provides the basis for certain types of empirical knowledge."[50] For example, Hume holds that without the influence of custom that determines us to believe in cause and effect, "we should be entirely ignorant of every matter of fact beyond what is immediately present to the memory and senses...There would be an end at once...of the chief part of speculation." Tweyman adds that, "without the natural belief in body, we should hold no beliefs about objects, and without the natural belief in personal identity, there would be no awareness of selfhood, and therefore, no beliefs about the self,"[51]

The second respect in which natural beliefs are important is that, "they provide us with essential ways of approaching our experience in order to get on in the world."[52] Concerning this second respect, Tweyman refers the reader to the *Enquiries,* where Hume writes:

> Here, then in a pre-established harmony between the course of nature and the succession of our ideas;...Custom is that principle, by which this correspondence has been effected; so necessary to the subsistence of our species, and regulation of our conduct, in every circumstance and occurrence of human life. Had not the presence of an object, instantly excited the idea of those objects, commonly conjoined with it, all our knowledge must have been limited to the narrow sphere of our memory and senses; and we should never

have been able to adjust means to ends, or employ our natural powers, either to the producing of good or avoiding of evil....(A)s this operation of mind, by which we infer like effects from like causes, and vice versa, is so essential to the subsistence of all human creatures, it is not probable, that it could be trusted to the fallacious deductions of our reason....[53]

Since we have a concern for "ourselves" in our interaction with the "world," Tweyman remarks that the cases of the continued and independent existence of the body and of personal identity are, "too manifest to require any elaboration here."[54]

I have now completed my exposition of Tweyman's account of Humean natural beliefs. Before turning to an evaluation of Tweyman's analysis of natural beliefs in its application to an "intelligent designer," I shall first examine certain passages from Parts III and XII of the *Dialogues* which are crucial in determining the adequacy of Tweyman's account.

In Part III of the *Dialogues* Cleanthes gives up on trying to argue according to "regular" causal argumentation, wherein "cause" and "effect" have been observed to be constantly conjoined in all past instances. Philo has blocked this approach as a possibility in arguing for God's existence. We have not observed universes in the making. Our universe is unique, and its putative cause is also unique. Therefore, we do not have the basis for an inference from the universe, taken as an effect, to its cause. Philo voices this objection in Part II of the *Dialogues*. It is the same objection Hume gives in the *Enquiry*. Philo raises other objections, but the chief one is the one that both "Philo" and Hume give.[55]

It is in the beginning of Part III that Cleanthes gives what have been referred to as his "illustrative analogies." He tells Philo that the similarity of works of nature to human art are "self-evident and undeniable," and that Philo's objections ought to be refuted "by illustrations, examples and instances rather than by serious argument and philosophy."[56] But instead of offering examples or instances taken from the natural world, Cleanthes initially offers some creative illustrations of his own devising. These are the well-known "articulate voice" and "vegetable library" illustrations. The text of the former "illustration" is as follows:

> "Suppose, (says Cleanthes)...that an articulate voice were heard in the clouds, much louder and more melodious than any which human art could ever reach; suppose that this voice were extended in the same instant over all nations and spoke to each nation in its own language and dialect; suppose that the words delivered not only contain a just sense and meaning, but convey some instruction altogether worthy of a benevolent Being superior to mankind—could you possibly hesitate a moment concerning the cause of this

voice, and must you not instantly ascribe it to some design and purpose?"[57]

When we hear an articulate voice in normal situations we infer that the voice proceeds from an intelligent cause, a person. But in the present case the voice is louder, more melodious, etc. This would indicate that it is produced by intelligence, but by an intelligence superior to a human being. The inference to a superior being, Cleanthes is suggesting, would be immediate. We would not require many repeated instances of such a phenomenon before we made the "inference." A single instance would suffice. Indeed, we would not make an *inference* at all. At least, we would not make an inference in the same sense that we would in regular cases of analogy. This is not an argument that Cleanthes is putting forth. By Cleanthes' own characterization of it, it is an example or an illustration of the "fact" that a design or purpose is "self-evident" in nature. Cleanthes takes the "articulate voice" to be self-evidently caused by intelligence and he thinks that we would stand in the same relation to the "articulate voice" as we stand in relation to the universe. But, in order to "bring the cases still nearer the present one of the universe," Cleanthes offers the illustration of the "vegetable library."[58] Suppose books perpetuated themselves like animals and vegetables, by generation and propagation. Could we open any such volume and hear it reason and discourse without immediately seeing that "its original cause bore the strongest analogy to mind and intelligence?"[59]

Hurlbutt says that the "library of vegetable books is similar in purport" to the "articulate voice."[60] I think he is correct in this. There are two objectives that Cleanthes has in giving these illustrations. First, Cleanthes seeks to circumvent the requirement of having to have observed the "origin of worlds" in order to make an inference from this world to its cause. This objective can be accomplished if Cleanthes can accomplish the second objective. The second objective is to illustrate the "fact" that a design or purpose is "self-evident" in nature, that it is intuitively obvious. If a design is intuitively obvious, then the unique instance of this present universe is sufficient to establish an intelligent designer as its cause, and, thus, to dispense with the need of having to observe many worlds in the making. This seems the most natural (in a non-Humean sense) interpretation of these "illustrative analogies." With regard to the "vegetable library" example, Cleanthes tells Philo that if there is any difference between this case and the case of the universe,

> ...it is all to the advantage of the latter. The anatomy of an animal affords many stronger instances of design than the perusal of Livy or Tacitus; and

any objection which you start in the former case, by carrying me back to...the first formation of worlds, the same objection has place on the supposition of our vegetating library.[61]

He then challenges Philo to assert either that a rational volume is no proof of rational cause, or that the universe has a rational cause.[62] This shows that Cleanthes believes that we would stand in the same relation to his "vegetable library" as we stand in relation to nature, and that in both cases an intelligent cause of design is "self-evident."

Cleanthes gives further examples in this section. When we consider the anatomy of the eye and "survey its structure and contrivance" the "idea of a contriver" will immediately flow in upon (us) with a force like that of sensation.[63] Consider the correspondence of the parts and instincts of males and females. It must make us sensible that "the propagation of the species is intended by nature."[64] Although these examples and illustrations were not originally characterized as "serious philosophical arguments," Cleanthes now calls them "natural arguments."[65] He says, "To what degree...of blind dogmatism must one have attained to reject such natural and convincing arguments?"[66] They may not be arguments which follow normal rules of induction (the Humean-Newtonian rules, as insisted on by Philo),[67] but we meet with "Some beauties in writing...which seem contrary to rules, (but) which gain the affections and animate the imagination in opposition to all the precepts of criticism...."[68] And the universal and irresistible influence of the argument for theism "prove(s) clearly that there may be arguments of a like irregular nature."[69]

Hurlbutt notes all these examples and illustrations and irregular arguments, and he points out that Hume talks about an "irregular" kind of reasoning that must be used in discovering certain relations between objects. Hume says, "Thus we may establish it as a maxim, that we can never, by any principle, but by an irregular kind of reasoning from experience, discover a connexion or repugnance betwixt objects..."[70] Hurlbutt reminds us that "natural propensities" play a significant role in Hume's position concerning skepticism.[71] He notes that, while external objects are not directly experienced, the "vulgar" and "those who hold to common sense" assume that objects are the cause of our impressions.[72] He also points out that qualities of the imagination, along with constancy and coherence in impressions, are what cause us to believe in independent objects, "and their uniform relations."[73] Quoting Hume, Hurlbutt relates that the "inference arises from the understanding and from custom in an indirect and oblique manner."[74]

Concerning Cleanthes' reference to "Some beauties in writing,"

Hurlbutt notes that Hume talks about "irregular writers" who transgress the "rules of art," and that the force of these writers' work has "the power to overcome censure."[75]

The illustrations and examples which are called "natural arguments" by Cleanthes all have the same purpose. They are meant to show that "the idea" of an intelligent cause of the universe is "self-evident." Hurlbutt takes these all together, I think, and refers to them as "the reformulated argument." He says, "My view is that the reformulated argument involves an appeal to natural propensity, or natural instinct; and does so in a way analogous to the views found in the *Treatise* and the *Enquiry Concerning Human Understanding.*"[76]

I think that Hurlbutt makes a good case for his view with regard to Cleanthes' position. But many theological writers of the time made appeals to natural instinct, or intuition, or self-evidence, or something of the kind.[77] At this point, there are two possibilities: (1) Hume himself held such a view, and he was expressing it in the *Dialogues,* or (2) Hume held no such view, but rather was attempting to capture a type of "argument" prevalent among design theorists of the time. The most we can say at present is that it is plausible to regard Cleanthes as holding that belief in an intelligent designer is something like a Humean "natural belief." But, even granting this much, it should be noted that Cleanthes does not say that the belief in an intelligent designer is essential to survival. Survival value, I shall argue, is criterial of unavoidable natural beliefs. One thing seems fairly clear. In the words of Tweyman, Cleanthes "holds an instinctive account of belief in an intelligent designer of the world."[78] It remains to be seen whether Cleanthes' account and Philo's account in Part XII are compatible.

Now, there is a prima facie case to be made for the idea that Cleanthes' instinctive account of belief in an "intelligent designer" in Part III is compatible with the "concessions" Philo appears to make in Part XII. They *may* both be *construed* as holding that such a belief is a natural one. But we will find that there are difficulties with this construal.

In part XII, Philo says that no one has a deeper sense of religion impressed on his mind than he.[79] He asks rhetorically whether it is possible for a God of which we have no sense impression to give stronger proofs of his existence than those found to appear "on the whole face of nature."[80] And I have already quoted Philo speaking about his profound adoration of the divine being and his suggestion that a skeptic will "fly to revealed truth." If we were antecedently convinced that Hume thought the belief in an "intelligent designer" was a "natural belief," then I think we would have no problem in construing Part XII as exemplifying such a position. But neither the *Dialogues* alone, nor Hume's other works alone can yield this position. All Hume's relevant comments about religion and belief must be taken in conjunction with what Philo and Cleanthes say in the *Dialogues*. If we do this we will find Tweyman's strong claim that the belief in an intelligent designer, "satisfies *all* the criteria of a natural belief, and, *therefore must* be regarded as being such a belief," cannot be accepted.[81]

I will argue presently that of Tweyman's six criteria for Humean "natural beliefs," (5) and (6) present the greatest difficulties for his account. However, before doing so, we can grant that (1) through (4) do apply to an intelligent designer, but granting this adds nothing whatsoever to Tweyman's argument. There is an open-ended list of beliefs that would satisfy criteria (1) through (4).

Criterion (1) is that a "natural belief" cannot be fully analyzed in terms of Hume's account of impressions and ideas. I think it will be granted that a belief in an intelligent designer of the world satisfies this criterion, but so do beliefs in witches, ghosts and goblins.[82] And these are clearly not candidates for consideration.

Criterion (2) says that the awareness accompanying a "natural belief" is substituted for the putative object of that belief. Again, we may "feign" anything we please and this feigned "awareness" may be substituted for its putative object. So, (2) would also apply to an open-ended list of beliefs.

Criterion (3) says that, for a "natural belief" we are unable to explicate its putative object. No one holds, for example, that the Christian Trinity is a "natural belief," but it is held by Christians that its putative object cannot be explicated; it is a "mystery." An extended list of beliefs also fits Criterion (3).

And, of course, the belief in an "intelligent designer" satisfies Criterion (4), which is that the putative object of a "natural belief" may not *be* at all. As Hume might say, "we can draw the inference for ourselves."

There is an immediate problem with Criterion (5), and Tweyman deals with this problem straightaway. As Tweyman says, the problem is that "...in Hume's writings on religion, there is an acknowledgement that the belief in an intelligent designer is not universal."[83] In the "Author's Introduction" to the *Natural History of Religion,* Hume says that there have been nations discovered who "entertained no sentiments of Religion, if travellers and historians may be credited."[84] The inference that Hume draws concerning this lack of religious sentiments in some nations is very instructive with respect to Tweyman's position. In his initial analysis of Humean "natural beliefs" he concluded his discussion of Criterion (5) (A Natural Belief is Unavoidable and Therefore Universal) by saying that, "We can see, therefore, that the unavoidability and universality of a given natural belief can be made manifest by showing the influence of instinct (Nature), and therefore, the impotence of skeptical arguments, in regard to this belief."[85]

But if we agree that it is plausible to regard the belief in an "intelligent designer" as a religious sentiment, then this passage in the *Natural History of Religion* can be seen as directly counter to Tweyman's position. Here is the relevant passage:

> The belief of invisible, intelligent power has been very generally diffused over the human race, in all places and in all ages; but it has neither perhaps been so universal as to admit of no exception, nor has it been, in any degree, uniform in ideas, which it has suggested. Some nations have been discovered, who entertained no sentiments of Religion, if travellers and historians may be credited; and no two nations, and scarce any two men, have ever agreed precisely in the same sentiments. It would appear, therefore, that this preconception springs not from an original instinct or primary impression of nature, such as gives rise to self-love, affection between the sexes, love of progeny, gratitude, resentment; since every instinct of this kind has been found *absolutely universal* in all nations and ages...[86]

I think this passage reveals two problems with Tweyman's view that belief in an "intelligent designer" is natural. The first problem concerns his claim that the universality of a natural belief can be "made manifest" by showing the influence of instinct. If a belief is instinctual, then we are determined by nature to hold that belief. This is true of the standard cases of natural beliefs. If we are determined by nature to hold a belief, then it is universal. This can be derived from Hume's argument in the quoted passage. Hume does hold that if a belief is instinctual, then it is universal. But he also holds that religious sentiments are not "absolutely universal." And his conclusion is that religious sentiments are not instinctual. Hume's argument has a modus tollens form. If we regard the belief in an "intelligent designer" as a religious sentiment, the argument is as follows: (1) If the belief in an "intelligent designer" is instinctual, then it is (absolutely) universal, (2) the belief in an "intelligent designer" is not (absolutely) universal, and the conclusion is (3) therefore, the belief in an "intelligent designer" is not instinctual. If the belief in an "intelligent designer" is neither instinctual nor universal, it fails to satisfy Criterion (5), so it is not a "natural belief." The only premise we needed to add to get this result was the quite plausible one that belief in an "intelligent designer" is a "religious sentiment." I claimed in the beginning of this chapter that Hume comes very close (at least) to explicitly denying that belief in an "intelligent designer" is a "natural belief." I believe that that claim has been adequately explained, and demonstrated to be correct.

Now, it might be argued that all I have succeeded in doing is to show that what Tweyman regards as a sufficient condition of universality does not hold in the case of an "intelligent designer." If showing that a belief is instinctual can "make manifest" its universality, then showing that a belief is instinctual is a sufficient condition for showing that belief's universality, but it need not be a necessary condition. Perhaps the universality of a belief can be shown in another way. Tweyman does argue for another way of showing this, in effect. But this is where Tweyman's second problem comes in (as revealed by the passage from the *Natural History of Religion*).

Tweyman's second problem, I believe, is that he misunderstands Hume's position regarding universality. This second problem cannot be demonstrated. It involves the question of whether we should regard Hume's "natural beliefs" as requiring what I should like to call "conditional universality," as opposed to "strict universality."

Tweyman gives a conditional analysis to universality in his initial treatment of an intelligent designer. He says, "Once it is understood that a natural belief for Hume is universal in the sense that there must be an experience of a certain kind for the belief to be generated, the universality of the belief in an intelligent designer is established."[87] His analysis does seem to go along with what Hume says about causality and the external world. But, it will be recalled, Hume rejected the idea that religious sentiments were instinctual because they were not "absolutely universal." Religious sentiments, Hume tells us, are not "so universal as to admit of no exceptions." It appears from this that he held to a strict standard of universality when considering whether religious sentiments were instinctual. Tweyman can be seen as misunderstanding this strict view, on the basis of his analysis of the standard cases of natural beliefs. I believe that Hume was consistent on this point, and that his own analysis of natural beliefs was not meant to imply that they were less than strictly universal.

In arguing for the conditional view of universality regarding an intelligent designer, Tweyman refers the reader back to Cleanthes' statement in Part III, where he is talking about being struck with a "force like that of sensation" when we "anatomize the eye" or consider the parts and instincts of males and females. The point of this, Tweyman says, is that "those who believe in an intelligent contriver are precisely the ones who have attended to the adjustments or adaptations of means to ends throughout nature."[88] This may be seen as helping to bring Cleanthes in line with Philo in Part XII. Tweyman says, "With our belief in an intelligent designer of the world Philo is equally clear: when we observe means to ends relations and coherence of parts, we are struck by the belief in intelligent contrivance."[89]

Evidence of this might be given by citing the opening page of Part XII, where Philo says that "A purpose, and intention, a design strike everywhere the most careless, the most stupid thinker," or we might cite Philo's reference to Galen on the next page, where he tells us that even this infidel could not withstand such striking appearances of design.[90]

Tweyman seeks to bring both Philo and Cleanthes in line with Hume by citing passages from Hume's *Natural History*. The first passage he cites is this:

> But a barbarous, necessitous animal (such as man is on the first origin of society) pressed by such numerous wants and passions, has no leisure to admire the regular face of nature, or make inquiries concerning the cause of those objects, to which from his infancy he has been gradually accustomed. On the contrary, the more regular and uniform, that is, the more perfect nature appears, the more he is familiarized to it, and the less inclined to scrutinize and examine it...an animal, complete in all its limbs and organs, is to him an ordinary spectacle, and produces no religious opinion or affectation. Ask him, whence that animal arose; he will tell you, from the copulation of its parents. And whence these? From the copulation of theirs. A few removes satisfy his curiosity, and set the objects at such a distance, that he entirely loses sight of them. Imagine not, that he will so much as start the question, whence the first animal; much less, whence the whole system, or united fabric of the universe.[91]

In this passage Hume maintains that our prehistoric ancestors did not ask questions concerning cosmogony. It is consistent with his view that religious sentiments are neither absolutely universal, nor instinctual. By itself it does not show that Hume accorded "natural beliefs" a status of "conditional universality" rather than "strict universality." But Tweyman follows this immediately with a second passage, which can, perhaps, be construed in this way. Hume says,

> Ignorant of astronomy and the anatomy of plants and animals, and too little curious to observe the admirable adjustment of final causes; they remain still unacquainted with a first and supreme creator, and with that infinitely perfect spirit, who alone, by his almighty will, bestowed order on the whole frame of nature.[92]

Now, this passage would seem to present a problem for my position. The last quoted passage suggests, although it does not necessitate, the view that "natural beliefs" are universal in a conditional sense. But it can also suggest that belief in an "intelligent designer" is based on argument, not instinct. If Hume is taken as suggesting that the belief in an intelligent designer is natural, then this would be inconsistent with his view that such a religious sentiment "springs not from an original instinct or primary impression of our nature." For it was rejected as such precisely because it was not strictly (Hume says "absolutely") universal. The first passage is not problematic, but the second passage may be. These passages, taken together with Cleanthes' remarks in Part III, Philo's remarks in Part XII, and the "conditional" view of universality that Hume appears to hold in the *Treatise* lead Tweyman to the conclusion that, "the issue of the universality of the belief in an intelligent designer for the world tends to dissolve."[93] However, this conclusion is not so easily arrived at. It would be a mistake to suppose that whether or not a belief was instinctual was not a very important consideration for Hume. I will have more to say on this point when I consider Tweyman's sixth criterion of natural beliefs. But for now it can be noted that our natural beliefs in the external world and causality were considered to be instinctual, and that these instinctive beliefs play a vital role in our survival as a species.[94] Given that they are "so necessary to the subsistence of our species" it seems implausible to think that Hume did not consider them to be strictly universal.

The solution to the problem, I believe, is to see Hume as taking it for granted that the conditions under which a natural belief arises are themselves universal. Hume thought that there would always be constancy and coherence in certain perceptions, and that we would always observe certain impressions to be constantly conjoined. This would reconcile the conditional analyses of "natural beliefs" that Hume does give with his view that "natural beliefs" *are instinctual* and universal. On this view, Hume was not giving a conditional analysis of *universality,* but rather he was giving an analysis of the conditions he thought prevailed in human life and an analysis of the natural responses of humans to those conditions. Nature determines that these conditions and responses both universally prevail.

In the "Author's Introduction" to the *Natural History of Religion,* Hume says that "this preconception springs not from an original instinct...of nature." The preconception he is talking about is the "belief of an invisible, intelligent power." And what he seems to be denying, by denying it is an original instinct, is that it is constitutive of human nature. This would be consistent with the implication of this passage that an "original instinct" is absolutely universal. An original instinct would be an instinct that Nature provides us with as constitutive of our own nature. This is one part of the reason why an original instinct *would* be found in all nations. The other part is that certain impressions will also be found to have been observed in all nations. I think that is a plausible way of interpreting Hume's meaning when he says that an original instinct is one which has "been found absolutely universal in all nations and ages, and has always a precise determinate object, which it inflexibly pursues."[95] I take it that they would not be considered to have precise determinate *objects* if constancy and coherence of impressions were absent. But since the original instincts are absolutely universal and they are always related to objects, the constancy and coherence of certain impressions (which is a necessary condition for "inferring" objects) must also be absolutely universal.

When I say that constancy and coherence of certain impressions are absolutely universal, I do not mean that the impressions are the same throughout the world. I mean only that some impressions will display these qualities throughout the world. Thus, the constancy and coherence of impressions which in part give rise to the belief in the existence of the "object" of my affection will differ from those which give rise to the belief in the existence of the "object" of another's affection in a different nation and age. But there will always be "objects of affection" in different nations and ages. So, there will always be constancy and coherence of certain impressions in different nations and ages.

If my position is consistent with Hume's other views, it perhaps has the merit of making explicable something that might otherwise be difficult to understand. This is the fact that Hume held that there "is a kind of pre-established harmony between the course of nature and the succession of our ideas..."[96] Nature determines, or pre-establishes, the constancy and coherence between certain perceptions, and the constant conjunction of certain of our impressions, on the one hand, and the response of natural belief, on the other. Custom effects the correspondence. And the act of mind by which it gives rise to our belief in the external world and causation is some "instinct or mechanical tendency" that nature has "implanted in us."[97] Since the instinct is vital to the survival of our species, it is constitutive of each member of the species, and so, absolutely universal.

I have argued that Hume explicitly denies that religious sentiments are instinctual, and therefore, he implicitly denies that a belief in an "intelligent designer" is instinctual. Although Tweyman holds, correctly I think, that the universality of a belief can be "made manifest" by showing it to be instinctual, he cannot show that the belief in an "intelligent designer" is universal in this way. I have also argued, against the position that "natural beliefs" are not absolutely universal, that (1) Hume adheres to a "strict" standard when rejecting religious sentiments as instinctual, i.e., they were rejected as instinctual precisely because they are not *absolutely* universal, but natural beliefs are instinctual and Hume should be regarded as consistently holding that they are also absolutely universal. And (2) it is implausible to regard "natural beliefs" as anything less than strictly universal, given that they are "so necessary to the subsistence of our species." With regard to (2) I have suggested that we should see Hume as regarding the conditions that give rise to "natural beliefs" as being themselves universal. This does justice to the fact that Hume does give a conditional analysis of "natural beliefs," and to the fact that he held that they are necessary for survival. What I hope the foregoing arguments tend to show is that even if Philo and Cleanthes are regarded as being compatible with each other on the view that belief in an intelligent designer is a natural belief, this is incompatible with Hume's position on that view, because it fails to satisfy the condition of universality that Hume places on natural beliefs.

Criterion (6) on Tweyman's list of criteria for Humean natural beliefs is that a natural belief is one which is "an affair of too great importance to be trusted to our uncertain reasonings and speculations." There are two respects in which he sees "natural beliefs" as being "an affair of too great importance" to be trusted to reason. They are: (1) A natural belief provides us with "the basis of certain types of empirical knowledge," and (2) it provides us with "essential ways of approaching our experiences in order to get on in the world."

With regard to the first respect, Tweyman says that, "Through the belief in an intelligent designer, an understanding of the presence of particular causes can be obtained in terms of the purpose which these causes assist in realizing." He holds that Philo takes this position in Part XII. The statement that Tweyman has in mind is this,

> That *'nature does nothing in vain,'* is a maxim established in all of the schools, merely from the contemplation of the works of nature, without any religious purpose; and from a firm conviction of its truth, an anatomist, who has a observed a new organ or canal, would never be satisfied till he had also discovered its use and intention.[98]

Tweyman holds that this passage implies that the belief in an intelligent designer is regarded by Philo as guiding the study of nature by establishing "the manner in which nature is to be studied."[99] And so the first respect in which natural beliefs are of "great importance" is held by Philo to be true of the belief in an intelligent designer.

Although I believe that what Tweyman deduces from Philo's statement about the "maxim" established in the schools is problematic, I would like to focus my attention on the second respect in which a natural belief is said to be of "great importance." The second respect is not treated in a way that does justice to Hume's position. Hume's position, or at least a very important part of it, is that natural beliefs are of such "great importance" because they are necessary to survival. Hume says that they are "necessary to the subsistence of our species."[100] The fact that Tweyman says that natural beliefs provide us essential ways of getting on in the world does seem to be consistent with this part of Hume's view, but in his explanation of what this means he seems to be making a much weaker claim for natural beliefs than Hume does. He states that the belief in an intelligent designer "has relevance to our search for causes."[101] He also states that such a belief "assists us in dealing with causes," but he goes on to say about this assistance that, "This is particularly useful in the context of scientific investigations of nature."[102] He quotes Philo as saying that "all the sciences *almost lead us insensibly* to acknowledge a first intelligent Author," and that they lay a strong foundation of piety and religion "without knowing it."[103]

He says all this in terms of giving support for the claim that belief in an intelligent designer is a natural belief in the second respect in which he sees natural beliefs as being of "great importance." But in the quotation from the *Enquiry* which he gives in his initial analysis of Criterion (6), in the second respect, Hume twice refers to the fact that custom-generated beliefs are necessary for our subsistence.[104] It is this that Hume is emphasizing in that passage, and Tweyman does not refer to it at all. Since our species survived throughout pre-scientific ages, custom-generated beliefs are pre-scientific. And, since they are pre-scientific, they have nothing necessarily to do with science at all. The "great importance" of natural beliefs (custom-generated beliefs) does not lie in their relation to science.

A further indication that the great importance of natural beliefs does not lie in their value in doing science is that the same natural beliefs that are "necessary to the subsistence of our species" are also found in other species. In the *Treatise,* Hume argues that animals learn from experience and that "inferences" concerning causes and effects are made in the same way that humans make them. He says,

> Beasts certainly never perceive any real connexion among objects. 'Tis therefore by experience they infer one from the other. They can never by any arguments form a general conclusion, that those objects, of which they have had no experience, resemble those of which they have. 'Tis therefore

by means of custom alone, that experience operates upon them.[105]

He reaffirms this view in the *Enquiry* by saying, among other things, that "it is custom alone, which engages animals, from every object, that strikes their senses, to infer its usual attendant..."[106]

I believe that what I have said, thus far, helps to show that the "great importance" of natural beliefs does not lie in their relation to science, although such a relation would add to their importance, but rather that it lies in their vital role in the survival of people and animals, in the survival of species. Insofar as Tweyman gives an explanation of the second respect in which he holds that a "natural belief" is important in terms of examples related to science, he suggests a weaker claim for "natural beliefs" than Hume himself appears to be making. The belief in an "intelligent designer" is claimed to be important in the *Dialogues* because it guides science in the achievement of empirical knowledge. Such knowledge could, in fact, enhance both our ability to survive and the quality of our lives, and this would be a respect in which that belief would be important. But since it would merely enhance the ability to survive, it would not be vital to survival. So even though it would be important, it would not be of such "great importance" as that which Hume ascribes to instinctual beliefs (custom-generated "natural beliefs"). The result is that a weaker claim is being made for an "intelligent designer" as an instinctive belief, than Hume makes for instinctive belief. For Tweyman, if we extrapolate from what he says about an "intelligent designer," natural beliefs are useful and so important, but not necessary, to our survival. For Hume, they were of "too great importance" to our survival to be unnecessary.

So far I have argued that the belief in an intelligent designer is neither instinctual nor universal, and so it fails to satisfy Criterion (5). I have also argued that a weaker claim is being made for Criterion (6) than Hume himself would make. I now want to argue for the position that Tweyman has not considered all the features of a natural belief. A seventh criterion should be added to Tweyman's list. It is, "A Belief Which Is A Natural Belief Is One Which Is Shared By Humans And Animals." When I was arguing concerning Tweyman's Criterion (6), I claimed that we share "natural beliefs" with animals. I have quoted Hume saying that animals have a belief in causality.

Hume also makes the claim that animals share the belief in "an external universe." He says in the *Enquiry*:

> It seems evident, that men are carried, by a natural instinct or prepossession, to repose faith in their senses; and that, without any reasoning we always

suppose an external universe, which depends not on our perception, but would exist, though we and every sensible creature were absent or annihilated. Even the animal creations are governed by a like opinion, and preserve this belief of external objects in all their thoughts, designs, and actions.[107]

Now, Hume's analysis of the "self" was problematic by his own account, and it is not clear that he ever felt that he solved his problem with it. He does seem to have wanted to give a similar account of "self" that he gave of the other natural beliefs, but this is only sketched in a little bit when it comes to the belief of "self" in animals. He says in Book II of the *Treatise* that, "The very port and gait of a swan, or turkey, or peacock show the high idea he has entertained of himself, and his contempt for all others."[108] He does this in the context of explaining his position that pride and humility are passions that are present in "almost every species of creatures."[109]

Norman Kemp Smith remarks on these and related passages and says that Hume does not give any attempt to "define more precisely the modes in which the idea of self enters, in the case of animals, either into the thought of the 'object' of the passions or the 'subjects' of them."[110] Nevertheless, Hume seems to have maintained that at least some other species also had an idea of the "self."

The "fact" that animals shared the beliefs in causality, the external world, and self, was a very important consideration for Hume. He thought of this fact as lending support to his theory concerning the nature of these beliefs. In the *Treatise* he says,

> The common defect of those systems, which philosophers have employ'd to account for the actions of the mind, is, that they suppose such a subtility and refinement of thought, as not only exceeds the capacity of mere animals, but even of children and the common people in our own species...Such a subtility is a clear proof of the falsehood, as the contrary simplicity of the truth, of any system.[111]

The importance of this consideration was not altered in the *Enquiry*. Hume says,

> ...any theory, by which we explain the operations of the understanding, or the origin and connexion of the passions in man, will acquire additional authority, if we find, that the same theory is requisite to explain the same phenomena in all other animals.[112]

Hume thought his theory was requisite. From all this I think it will be seen to be plausible to add, as a seventh criterion of Humean "natural beliefs," that, "A Belief Which Is A Natural Belief Is One Which Is Shared By Humans And Animals." But if it is plausible to add this criterion, then it is implausible to count the belief in an intelligent designer as a natural belief, since, presumably, the belief in an intelligent designer is not shared by animals. Inasmuch as Hume thought that our prehistoric ancestors did not possess this belief, he would hardly think that animals possessed it. As far as I know, neither Hurlbutt nor Tweyman consider animals in their accounts of Humean natural beliefs.

I have argued that the belief in an intelligent designer is (1) not instinctual, (2) not universal in the strict sense of universal which Hume applies, (3) not necessary for survival and so is not of as "great importance" as, say, the belief in causality and (4), unlike the natural beliefs, it is not shared by animals.

# Chapter I

## Notes

1. David Hume, *Dialogues Concerning Natural Religion*, ed. Henry D. Aiken (New York: Hafner Press, 1984), p. 82.

2. Ibid., p. 94.

3. David Hume, *Dialogues Concerning Natural Religion*, ed. Norman Kemp Smith (Indianapolis: Thomas Nelson and Sons Ltd., 1947), p. 26.

4. Frederick Copplestone, *A History of Philosophy*, vol. 5 (New York: Image Books, 1985), p. 308. Copplestone quotes a 1751 letter from Hume to Sir Gilbert Elliot in which Hume tells Elliot that he makes Cleanthes the hero and asks Elliot for comments which would strengthen Cleanthes' position.

5. Robert Hurlbutt, *Hume, Newton and the Design Argument* (Lincoln: University of Nebraska Press, 1985), p. 215.

6. Stanley Tweyman, *Scepticism and Belief in Hume's* Dialogues Concerning Natural Religion (Dordrecht: Martinus Nyhoff Publishers, 1986), p. 132.

7. Robert Hurlbutt, *Hume*, pp. 222–231; C.G. Prado, "Hume And The God-Hypothesis," *Hume Studies* 7, no. 2 (November 1981): p. 162. Prado says that he is "sympathetic" to the view that "Hume thinks that a 'vague deism' is a natural belief"; H. S. Harris, "The 'Naturalness' of Natural Religion," *Hume Studies* 7, no. 1 (April 1987): p. 11. Harris says, "The unifying thesis of Hume's *Dialogues* is that religious belief is natural."

8. Norman Kemp Smith, *The Philosophy of David Hume* (London: Macmillan and Co. Ltd., 1947), p. 455. Smith holds that belief in causality and the belief in an external world are the only "natural beliefs"; Pheroze Wadia, "Philo Confounded," *McGill Hume Studies*, p. 290. Wadia quotes a letter from Hume to Gilbert Elliot where Hume states that the "propensity" to draw the inference of the design argument is "not as strong and universal as that to believe in our senses and experience." Wadia's comment on Hume's remark is, "This is one more nail in the coffin of the view held by some that Hume thought of belief in God as 'unavoidable' on the model of his doctrine of 'natural belief'"; B.O.A. Williams, "Hume on Religion," *David Hume: A Symposium* (New York: Macmillan & Co., Ltd., 1963), p. 81. Williams maintains that, "...it is certain that Hume did not regard religious belief as natural, in his special sense of that term—that is, as something which human nature, by its very constitution, must embrace..."

9. Tweyman, *Scepticism*, pp. 121–146. The independent analysis runs from p. 10 to p. 19.

10. Hurlbutt, *Hume*, p. 222.

11. Tweyman, *Scepticism*, p. 132.

12. Ibid.

13. Ibid., p. 132.

14. Antony Flew remarks on the impossibility of deducing Hume's views directly from the *Dialogues:* "Since the *Dialogues* are indeed dialogues...it is no more possible to deduce Hume's personal position directly from this text than we can deduce Shakespeare's political and religious convictions from his plays." Antony Flew, *David Hume: Philosopher of Moral Science* (New York: Basil Blackwell Ltd., 1986), p. 67. While I agree with Flew regarding Hume's position on natural belief, it is clear from the *Dialogues* that Hume does not think that the design argument proves a benevolent, all-powerful designer.

15. Tweyman, *Scepticism*, p. 11.

16. Ibid., pp. 12–17.

17. Ibid., pp 12.

18. Ibid., p. 12; Hume, *A Treatise of Human Nature*, ed. Selby-Bigge and P.H. Nidditch (Oxford: Oxford University Press, 1980), p. 5.

19. Hume, *Treatise*, ed. Selby-Bigge, p. 3.

20. Ibid., p. 96.

21. Hume may have a problem here. Very simply put, the problem is this: If beliefs are "lively ideas" and ideas must have corresponding impressions, then "natural beliefs" (which have no corresponding impressions) are not "lively ideas." If natural beliefs are not lively ideas, then they are not natural beliefs. In the Appendix, Hume makes belief "a peculiar feeling, different from the simple conception," p. 624.

22. Although I believe that Tweyman is right to include personal identity as a natural belief, it is not "non-controversial." Norman Kemp Smith argues that, "Natural belief takes two forms, as belief in continuing and therefore independent existence, and as a belief in causal dependence. It is these beliefs and these alone, in their generality, which are irresistible." Norman Kemp Smith, *The Philosophy of*

*David Hume*, p. 455. Add to this that Hume was not satisfied with his analysis of personal identity. He did seem to want to treat personal identity as a natural belief, but he had problems in treating it in the same way as the others. In the *Treatise*, Hume states that, "'Tis evident, that the idea, or rather the impression of ourselves is always intimately present with us...," ed. Selby-Bigge, pp. 317–18.

23. Tweyman, *Scepticism*, pp. 12–13; Hume, *Treatise*, ed. Selby-Bigge, pp. 251–252.

24. Hume, *Treatise*, ed. Selby-Bigge, p. 252.

25. Tweyman, *Scepticism*, p. 13.

26. Ibid.

27. Hume, *Treatise*, ed. Selby-Bigge, p. 252.

28. Ibid.

29. Ibid., p. 187.

30. Tweyman, *Scepticism*, pp. 13–14.

31. Hume, *Treatise*, ed. Selby-Bigge, p. 165.

32. Ibid., p. 156.

33. Tweyman, *Scepticism*, p. 14.

34. Hume, *Treatise*, ed. Selby-Bigge, p. 157.

35. Ibid., p. 167.

36. Ibid., p. 208.

37. My purpose is not to take Hume up on the many problems that arise in his various analyses of "natural beliefs." What, for example, does it mean to "feign," precisely?

38. Tweyman, *Scepticism*, p. 15.

39. Hume, *Treatise*, ed. Selby-Bigge, p. 209.

40. Ibid., p. 260.

41. Tweyman, *Scepticism*, p. 15.

42. Ibid.

43. Ibid.

44. Tweyman, *Scepticism*, p. 16; Hume, *Treatise*, ed. Selby-Bigge, p. 187.

45. Ibid.

46. Hume, *Treatise*, ed. Selby-Bigge, p. 194.

47. Tweyman, *Scepticism*, p. 16.

48. Ibid., p. 17; Hume, *Enquiries Concerning Human Understanding and Concerning the Principles of Morals*, ed. L.A. Selby-Bigge (Oxford: Oxford University Press, 1980), pp. 158–159.

49. Ibid.

50. Ibid.

51. Hume, *Enquiry*, p. 145; Tweyman, *Scepticism*, p. 17.

52. Tweyman, *Scepticism*, p. 18.

53. Hume, *Enquiry*, p. 55.

54. Ibid.

55. *Dialogues*, ed. Aiken, p. 23. *Enquiry*, p. 148.

56. Hume, *Dialogues*, ed. Aiken, p. 26.

57. Ibid.

58. Ibid.
59. Ibid.
60. Hurlbutt, *Hume*, p. 221.
61. Hume, *Dialogues*, ed. Aiken, p. 28.
62. Ibid.
63. Ibid.
64. Ibid.
65. Ibid.
66. Ibid.
67. Hurlbutt, *Hume*, p. 147. Also, Antony Flew shows the distinct similarities between Hume and Newton on rules of induction. Flew, *Hume's Philosophy of Belief* (New York: Humanities Press, 1961), p. 225.
68. Hume, *Dialogues*, ed. Aiken, p. 28.
69. Ibid.
70. Hurlbutt, *Hume*, p. 222; *Treatise*, ed. Selby-Bigge, p. 242.
71. Ibid. On "natural propensities" he refers the reader to the *Treatise*, ed. Selby-Bigge, pp. 183–187 and the *Enquiry*, pp. 151–165.
72. Ibid. The reference given is to the *Treatise*, ed. Selby-Bigge, pp. 193, 269–273.
73. Ibid., p. 223. His references are to the *Treatise*, ed. Selby-Bigge, pp. 150, 193, 197–215, 242 and 269–273.
74. Ibid. *Treatise*, ed. Selby-Bigge, p. 197.
75. Ibid. The writers are poets. The reference is to Hume's essay, "The Standard of Taste."
76. Ibid., p. 222.
77. Hurlbutt himself makes the case for this particular point (Ibid., pp. 141–143), although he later changed his mind on what was going on in the *Dialogues* as a whole. His present view concerning natural belief in an intelligent designer is given in an appendix to the revised 1985 edition of *Hume, Newton and the Design Argument*. The appendix is in the form of an essay entitled, "The *Dialogues* as a Work of Art."
78. Tweyman, *Scepticism*, p. 64.
79. Hume, *Dialogues*, ed. Aiken, p. 82.
80. Ibid., p. 83.
81. Tweyman, *Scepticism*, p. 132. Emphasis added.
82. John O. Nelson makes a similar comment with regard to Cleanthes' "irregular" inference or "natural argument" in Part III. He says that Cleanthes' claim that when we "anatomize the eye," the idea of a contriver will flow in upon us "with a force like that of a sensation..." "can also be used to infer goblins...on a dark, stormy night in a strange forest." "The Role of Part XII in Hume's *Dialogues Concerning Natural Religion*," *Hume Studies* 14, no. 2 (November 1988), p. 370, n. 13.
83. Tweyman, *Scepticism*, p. 136.
84. Hume, *Natural History of Religion*, ed. H. E. Root, (Stanford: Stanford University Press, 1956), p. 21.

85. Tweyman, *Scepticism*, p. 17.
86. Hume, *Natural History of Religion*, p. 21. Emphasis added.
87. Tweyman, *Scepticism*, p. 139.
88. Ibid., p. 137.
89. Ibid., p. 136.
90. Hume, *Dialogues*, ed. Aiken, pp. 82–83.
91. Tweyman, *Scepticism*, pp. 137–138; Hume, *Natural History*, pp. 24–25.
92. Ibid.; Hume, *Natural History*, p. 30.
93. Ibid., p. 138.
94. Hume, *Enquiry*, pp. 54–55.
95. Hume, *Natural History*, p. 21.
96. Hume, *Enquiry*, p. 54.
97. Ibid., p. 55.
98. Tweyman, *Scepticism*, p. 142; Hume, *Dialogues*, ed. Aiken, p. 82.
99. Ibid.
100. Hume, *Enquiry*, p. 55.
101. Tweyman, *Scepticism*, p. 145.
102. Ibid.
103. Ibid.
104. Ibid, p. 18; Hume, *Enquiry*, p. 55.
105. Hume, *Treatise*, ed. Selby-Bigge, p. 178.
106. Hume, *Enquiry*, p. 106.
107. Ibid., p. 151.
108. Hume, *Treatise*, ed. Selby-Bigge, p. 326.
109. Ibid.
110. Norman Kemp Smith, *The Philosophy of David Hume*, p. 109.
111. Hume, *Treatise*, p. 177.
112. Hume, *Enquiry*, p. 82.

# Chapter II

## "Strong" vs. "Weak" Natural Belief and *Dialogue* XII

In the previous chapter, I have argued that the belief in an intelligent designer is (1) not instinctual, (2) not universal in the strict sense of universal that Hume applies, (3) not necessary for survival and so not of as "great importance," as, for example, the belief in causality, and (4) that, unlike the universally held "natural beliefs," it is not shared by animals. This has paved the way for a different interpretation of Philo's remarks in Part XII of the *Dialogues,* since it is now, I take it, implausible to regard Hume as trying to convey the message that belief in an intelligent designer is a natural one in his special sense of a "natural belief."

Hurlbutt's treatment of the *Dialogues* as art demonstrates that Hume was expressing many different feelings, attitudes, positions, etc. I believe that Hume was combating what he regarded as the "superstition and fanaticism" of popular religion by showing that proofs are impossible in natural theology, and also by showing that anthropomorphic assumptions lead to absurdity. In addition, I believe he was expressing a view of the tenacity of these assumptions through all three of the characters participating in the discussion. In a recent treatment of the *Dialogues,* Hurlbutt says

> ...he (Hume) indicates that the projection of the concept of intelligent design upon features of the world is irresistible, perhaps as irresistible as belief in an external world, uniformity and causality, and in the general efficacy of reason and the senses.[1]

Although I disagree with Hurlbutt's suggestion for reasons already stated, I cannot help but think that Hurlbutt, et al, have a useful point to make in this regard. It is that, for Hume, the concept of intelligent design was virtually irresistible, but that this design was thought to originate from within "nature" itself.

Now, I would like to turn to Part XII and give a reading of it that I think accords well with the attack on "superstition and fanaticism" in the *Natural History of Religion,* and that also accords well with the genesis of religious belief as it is explained in that work. It is a limited analysis, and it does not resolve all the difficulties, but I think it will be seen to be plausible. I believe it does justice both to the insights of Hurlbutt, Tweyman, et al, and to Hume's own propensity for irony, while laying the groundwork which will enable us to see what Hume's own religious position was.

In Part XII of Hume's *Dialogues,* Philo says that no one has a deeper sense of religion than he and that no one "pays more profound adoration to the Divine Being, as he discovers himself to reason..."[2] The last part of this quotation ("as he discovers himself to reason") has to be kept in mind as an important indication of what it is that Philo commits himself to.

It might be thought that Philo gives everything away here and that Hume's theism finally expresses itself through the one dialogue participant who has resisted theism throughout the course of the work. This expression of Hume's theism, it may be maintained, is substantial at the end of the dialogue, where Pamphilus sums up his impressions of the discussion. Pamphilus says "...Philo's principles are more probable than Demea's, but....those of Cleanthes approach still nearer to the truth."[3]

Whether Hume means a bit of dialogue to be ironic or not, the last section actually strengthens Philo's previous position against Cleanthes. Philo has allowed all along that there seems to be some evidence of design in the universe. In a previous section where Philo "marks the consequences" of Cleanthes' argument from design, he says that there may be more than one deity or that the deity may be infantile, or senile, that the universe may be the last in a long series of trial and error attempts.[4] But he doesn't give up the idea of design in doing this, and Cleanthes is able to claim that the foundation of religion is still in place.

So, what does Philo commit himself to in the last section? Toward the end of it, Philo claims that skepticism is but the first step on the road to becoming "a sound, believing Christian." Although it appears that Philo gives the store to Cleanthes, it may be one of the most stinging ironies of the whole work.

Prior to this statement, in virtually all of the previous material, Philo argues against anthropomorphism. Now Philo is claiming that a person with a "just sense" of the imperfections of reason will "fly to revealed truth" in order to fill in the gaps in his apprehension of the divine.

If this is not irony, then Philo (Hume) has not "marked the

consequences" of statements immediately preceding this statement of faith. On the page prior to this statement, Philo says that it would be absurd to believe that the deity has human passions, and at the end of the very next paragraph, he states that philosophical skeptics "from a natural diffidence of their own capacity" endeavor to suspend judgment on the extraordinary subject of the divine perfections. I think that it is fair to take the person with a "just sense" of the imperfections of reason and the philosophical skeptic as one and the same.

In the statements under discussion then, Philo is talking about himself. It is he, of course, who thinks that the attribution of human passions to the deity is absurd. It is he who is the skeptic with a natural diffidence of his own capacity and it is he, as a "philosophical skeptic" and man of letters, who will fly to revealed truth. This is a source of the perplexity involved in understanding Part XII

One more preliminary consideration is in order before we can see the possibility that there is great irony in the idea that skepticism is the first step toward being a "sound, believing Christian." Philo does not elaborate on the concept of revelation. Although Philo does not say it, the text licenses taking "revelation" to refer to the biblical rendition central to Christianity. It is traditionally taken to be a communication from a transcendent agent. Revelation may have a source other than the Bible. This is possible. Philo refers to revelation as an "adventitious instructor." For Cleanthes, an anthropomorphite who defends religion as a whole, the "adventitious instruction" would probably come mainly from the Bible. It seems more likely that Philo is referring to Cleanthes' model of revelation.

Now the Bible is either absurd, or it depicts absurdities, according to Philo, because it portrays God as a being with passions such as anger, jealousy, etc. Maybe true revelation has to be sorted out, but Philo does not say this. The opposite suggestion is made when it is said that the reason for flying to revelation is an awareness of the imperfections of natural reason. Revelation, it seems, informs reason but is not judged by it.

Now let us "mark the consequences." Philo says a skeptic will fly to revelation. He also says that it is absurd to believe that the deity has human passions. Revelation depicts a deity with passions analogous to human passions, therefore, revelation is absurd. To fly to revelation is to be a "sound, believing Christian," because to be a sound, believing *Christian* requires acceptance of revelation. Therefore, to be a "sound, believing Christian" is to accept absurdity.

In order to see Philo's closing remarks as possibly being ironic, I have had to provide two propositions not explicitly stated in the text. The first one is that "revelation" refers to the Bible. The second one is that the Bible depicts the deity as having passions such as jealousy and anger. The first proposition seems warranted by the text. Philo has been talking with two Christians. For Christians, "revelation" can refer exclusively to the Bible. Catholics have another source of revelation, however. In the Catholic tradition it is held that continuing revelation is mediated by the church, as a further elaboration of the Bible. But this would be anthropomorphic too, and as such it would be considered "vulgar superstition" by Philo. So, even if this ongoing tradition is included in Philo's concept of revelation, it still contains the anthropomorphism that Philo considers absurd. Although I think that he is not including the Catholic tradition of revelation in his conception, it would not alter my conclusion if he did.

The result of these considerations seems to be that the philosophical skeptic, in order to be a sound, believing Christian, would have to fly to absurdity. I doubt that Hume missed this, and so I think it probable that the flight to revelation is intended to be ironic, that is, it is not intended to be taken at face value. Hume attacks superstition in the *Natural History of Religion,* but he never directly criticizes the Bible. Here he can be seen as suggesting that it is full of superstitions.

The question remains, "What is Philo committed to, given the last section of the *Dialogue?*" Philo says that,

> If the whole of natural theology,...resolves itself into one simple, though somewhat ambiguous, at least undefined, proposition, that the cause or causes of order in the universe probably bear some remote analogy to human intelligence...,

then we can do no more than believe that the arguments in favor outweigh the arguments against it.[5] This is all that reason can allow. For more than this, e.g., whether there be more than one cause, or one cause only, or whether the cause or causes have other characteristics that are analogous to human beings, like passions, we must "fly to revelation." But that would be absurd, so we are left with roughly the same position that Philo has held all along, viz., there may be some remote analogy to human intelligence in the cause or causes of order in the universe.

Philo does seem to think that there is only one cause of the order in the universe. He refers to God, or Divine Being, and not to gods or divine beings. But, short of revelation, there seems to be no reason to attribute human characteristics, other than intelligence, to God. If Philo sees the flight to revelation as absurd, then Philo is not a traditional theist. Traditional monotheism attributes human passions to God, magnified of course, and Philo will have none of this. The flight to the revelation of a God with various passions is an excursion into superstition.

So, while there does seem to be a belief in a "divine intelligence," the traditional Christian monotheistic conception of God is not the conception held by Philo. It is possible that Philo is a deist (that Hume is a deist). This would save Philo from having to believe in miracles, such as are depicted in the Bible. Revelation itself would be an instance of a miracle. As a violation of the laws of nature, miracles are at least highly improbable and perhaps even impossible, for Hume.[6] A deistic conception of God is one in which god created the laws of nature and then let the universe run along without interference according to those laws. So, deism is a possibility for Hume.

It is also possible that Philo was a pantheist, and, by implication, that Hume was a pantheist. Philo argues, in an earlier part of the dialogue, that the "divine intelligence" could be immanent, i.e., that the universe could possess the principle of order within itself. In this case, the "divine intelligence" would be the "soul" of the universe, it would be its immanent animating and ordering principle. Philo says of the universe, "By supposing it to contain the principle of its order within itself, we really assert it to be God; and the sooner we arrive at the Divine Being, so much the better."[7]

These two possibilities, that of deism and of pantheism, would probably be seen as useless ones by Hume. They are both consistent with the proposition that the cause of order bears some analogy with human intelligence, but they both depict the deity, whether transcendent or immanent, as being uninterested in human affairs. And Philo holds that, "...if it (the stated proposition) affords no inference that effects human life, or can be the source of any action or forbearance..." we can only give philosophical assent to it, but beyond that we would derive no guidance in ethics, no hope of future reward, and no basis for further explanations of phenomena.[8] In a practical sense such beliefs would be useless. But in order for God to take an interest, he would have to have passions. So, useless beliefs may be all that reason allows.

We have arrived at this point, in part, by way of rejecting the view that the belief in an intelligent designer of the universe is natural, for Hume, and that this view gets expressed in the *Dialogues*. I now want to reconsider that view in light of a distinction between different kinds of Humean natural beliefs. The irony in the *Dialogues* seems patent. But what we might call the "ironic interpretation" of Part XII (and we can distinguish several versions of this) is notoriously unsatisfactory as a complete explanation of Philo's moves in Part XII to those who hold the "natural belief interpretation" of that section. This latter interpretation is held by not a few philosophers, and not without reason. I will now endeavor to explain what it is that is right and what it is that is wrong with this interpretation.

The question is whether the belief in an intelligent designer of the universe is being treated as a natural belief in the *Dialogues*. It has been argued by Stanley Tweyman, and others, that this is the import of Part XII; that this is the way to understand what is going on with Philo's "concessions" to religion in Part XII, in statements about the skeptic flying to revealed truth, about a design being evident in nature, and so forth. Hume is expressing the view, through Philo, as he had already done through Cleanthes, that the belief in an intelligent designer is a natural belief, it is not something that can be proven (just as belief in objective existence cannot be proven) but nevertheless, it is a belief that one cannot help but maintain.

Tweyman argues that the belief in an intelligent designer satisfies all the criteria that are applicable to other or "non-controversial" Humean natural beliefs. Therefore, the belief in an intelligent designer is also a natural belief. He does this through an independent analysis of Hume's natural beliefs and then compares what Hume says about belief in an intelligent designer, mainly through the characters in the *Dialogues,* and he concludes that the belief in an intelligent designer satisfies all the criteria applicable to the non-controversial cases of natural beliefs.

According to this position, what is happening in Part XII is that Hume is expressing the view that regardless of the fact that the design argument fails as a regular argument from analogy, the conclusion of the design argument is actually a natural belief. There is a human propensity to believe in intelligent design prior to any argumentation.

It wouldn't do to regard Philo as suddenly endorsing the design argument, an argument that he has shown to be hopelessly weak. It seems that a more plausible view, given the decisive undermining of the design argument, is to say that Philo/Hume is not suddenly now accepting the design argument. Rather he is expressing the fact, or the alleged fact, that the belief in the argument's conclusion (that there is an intelligent designer) is a natural belief. We cannot argue in such a way as to demonstrate the truth of an intelligent designer's existence. Hume/Philo has not changed his view on this, but rather he is saying that the conclusion, as a belief per se, is natural.

To a certain extent, Cleanthes had taken such a position. At least, it can be argued that he had taken such a position.[9] Philo certainly says that design is evident in nature. This view would not require us to see Hume/Philo as suddenly endorsing an argument that has been shown by himself (either Hume or Philo) to be hopelessly weak. This gives the natural belief interpretation of Part XII some plausibility.

Another possible interpretation that has some initial plausibility is that there are two arguments that Cleanthes is giving, the first version in Part II and the second version in Part III.[10] Part II argues according to what, in the context of the *Dialogues,* are considered to be regular rules of analogical reasoning. But Philo blocks this approach by saying that, according to regular rules of analogical reasoning, one must have seen causes and effects at work before inferring from this particular effect or cause to its cause or effect, and as a matter of fact we have not observed worlds in the making (worlds being the effect and whatever makes them being the cause). We have not observed this and so we cannot infer from this world, taken as an effect, to its cause. So according to the regular rules of inductive reasoning, according to Philo, we cannot draw the conclusion that there is an intelligent designer of this universe. But in Part III, Cleanthes gives his illustrative analogies, the articulate voice from the sky and the vegetable library, and he argues that we would stand in the same relation to the articulate voice coming from the sky as we *do* stand in relation to the universe. In both cases he is illustrating, according to Cleanthes' own characterization of this, the fact that we would see it as immediately obvious that the source of the articulate voice is intelligent. And, by parity of reasoning, since we stand in the same relation to the universe as we would stand in relation to the articulate voice, we can see as immediately obvious that the universe's source is intelligent.[11]

Cleanthes, in Part III, says that Philo's cavils should be addressed by stating facts and giving illustrations, and then he goes on to provide creative illustrations of his own devising. He does not cite facts from nature originally, although later in the same section he says that when we anatomize the eye, the idea of an intelligent designer will strike us. But initially he says that he is not really giving an argument, he is just illustrating self-evident fact. And this would be question-begging *as an argument.*

But, what is Cleanthes doing here? If he is successful in demonstrating the self-evident fact of intelligent design, then he does not need to have observed universes in the making. If it is intuitively obvious from the presence of this universe that it is intelligently designed, as it would be intuitively obvious that the articulate voice from the clouds was intelligent or had an intelligent source, then we do not need to have observed universes in the making. The presence of this universe is sufficient to infer the existence of a designer. So he circumvents Philo's objection to the argument given in Part II. The argument given in Part II will not work because it tries to proceed by "regular" rules of argumentation, analogical rules. But it cannot succeed because it does not have the necessary data to go by: the observation of *constant conjunction* between worlds coming into existence and the causes of their doing so.

But now Cleanthes claims in Part III that one does not really need such data, neither does one need an argument. Design simply requires pointing out. But if one wants something more, imagine these cases of the articulate voice and the vegetable library. It should be immediately obvious that they are intelligent or they have intelligent sources and we stand in the same relation with them as we stand in relation with the universe. So Cleanthes is taking the view that belief in an intelligent designer is natural, does not need an argument and is intuitively obvious to us.

It is the existence of a designer which is claimed to be intuitively obvious, not the design argument. I do not think he is giving another argument, but it has been maintained that this is a second version of the argument. And it is true that after initially putting it forth not as an argument, but as an illustration of self-evident fact, Cleanthes characterizes it as a "natural argument" and asks Philo what degree of dogmatism must be maintained in order to reject such natural, irresistible arguments. So one can regard this as a second version of the argument and then say with regard to Part XII that Philo *is being consistent*. He never really answers Cleanthes in Part III. He is "confounded," dumbfounded, perhaps, as one might be[12]. In an actual situation like this someone might be dumbfounded and not know *what* to say. In any case, Philo does not say anything. But then in Part XII, Philo seems to be accepting some version of the design argument.

It has been suggested that Philo is accepting the *second version* of the argument, and so, being consistent, he is consistently rejecting the first version, so there is no inconsistency in Philo's "concession" to religion at the conclusion of the *Dialogues*. This position has some initial plausibility because it would make Philo consistent on the question of whether he accepts or rejects the argument. He rejects one version and he accepts the other. Nevertheless, this position must get over the objection that this would be to say that Philo is accepting a question-begging argument. It is neither likely that Hume failed to see Cleanthes' illustrations as question-begging arguments, nor that he would want Philo to accept a question-begging argument. On the other hand, if one simply held that Philo is accepting the statement "there is an intelligent designer," and accepting *that* belief as a natural one, then this view of Part XII seems to be more plausible. One problem with this is that there is some ambiguity in the term "natural belief." If we mean that the belief in an intelligent designer is absolutely universal, having the same status as the belief in objects or causal relations between objects, then it is not a natural belief.

Hume did have a view of religious beliefs as being based on some element of human nature, which he called a "secondary principle" in the *Natural History of Religion*.[13] He differentiates between primary impressions, or instincts of human nature, and secondary principles and he says that the objects of "primary" instincts or impressions are universal and these are such as give rise to affection between the sexes, love of progeny and other relations.[14] These are universal, but secondary principles are such as can be prevented. There are some nations that have not had religious sentiments "if travelers and historians can be credited."[15] He seems to credit them. He draws the inference that the belief in an invisible intelligent power cannot be based on a primary instinct because it is not absolutely universal.[16] So he says that it must be some secondary principle in human nature.

My position, then, is that it is not the case that Philo is accepting some version of an argument for an intelligent designer of the universe in Part XII. Nor is it the case that Philo and Cleanthes together, that is to say Hume, through his characters, is expressing the view that belief in an intelligent designer is a natural belief in a "primary" sense of natural belief, where this belief has the same status as belief in objective existence and belief in causation between objects.[17] But we can distinguish that primary sense from a secondary sense and call it "strongly natural" (a *strong* natural belief would be strictly universal and it would be based on a primary instinct of human nature). A belief in causation between objects would be strongly natural. If we make a distinction between *strong* natural beliefs and *weak* natural beliefs, then I think that Tweyman, Hurlbutt and Harris have a point.[18] That is to say that as a matter of fact, belief in an invisible intelligent power is treated by Hume as a (weakly) natural belief in *The Natural History*. Not every one of us has this belief, but it has certainly been found in almost every nation and age. There have not been whole nations and ages that have been bereft of this belief, as Hume seems to think, but there have been individuals, and there seem always to have been individuals who did not accept this belief. Hume holds that this belief is not something that we are compelled to have by nature, by primary instinct. In that sense it is *not* strongly natural. A strong natural belief, on the model of the uncontroversial cases, would be *absolutely* universal. Hume holds that a belief in invisible, intelligent power is something that arises out of human nature or out of the human condition, that is to say out of the kind of experiences that we have, along with the propensities human nature is given to, even though it is not universal. In this sense it is "weakly natural."

Our original resistance to the idea that belief in an intelligent designer of the universe is natural for Hume was based on the objection that for Hume natural beliefs must be strictly universal, and belief in an intelligent designer is not absolutely universal. But we can relax this resistance once we distinguish between different senses of natural belief in the Humean corpus. The first sense of natural beliefs refers to beliefs which are strictly universal and invariable, the second sense refers to beliefs that are "generally diffused" but not completely universal and not invariable (they take various forms). Hume says,

> The belief of invisible, intelligent power has been very generally diffused over the human race, in all places and in all ages; but it has neither perhaps been so universal as to admit of no exception, *nor has it been, in any degree, uniform in the ideas, which it has suggested.* Some nations have been discovered, who entertained no sentiments of Religion, if travellers and historians may be credited; and no two nations, and scarce any two men, have ever agreed precisely in the same sentiments.[19]

The distinction between strongly natural and weakly natural beliefs in Hume, corresponds to Hume's distinction between primary instincts and beliefs based on those, and secondary principles of human nature and beliefs based on those. This distinction affords us an interpretation of Part XII that is consistent with the criticism of anthropomorphism both in the preceding Parts of the *Dialogues* and in the *Natural History,* as well as with Hume's account of the origin of religious belief in the *Natural History*.[20] We would not have to see Hume as trying to put forth the message with the *Dialogues* that religious belief is natural in the sense of having the same status as those which Tweyman calls the "non-controversial cases" of natural belief, that is to say: the status of belief in personal identity, belief in objects or objective existence and belief in causal relations between objects. It also allows us to see what is right about Tweyman's position on this issue.

Hurlbutt too sees that the way Hume seems to treat religious beliefs is in some sense analogous to the way he treats strong natural beliefs. But these beliefs which involve the idea of invisible intelligent power (the beliefs could be monotheistic, polytheistic, or animistic) are based on "secondary principles" of human nature. These principles do not *invariably* give rise to a belief in an intelligent designer of the universe. This belief is but one member of the class of beliefs in invisible, intelligent power. And not even the whole class is universal for Hume.

Tweyman argues that the objection from universality, from the fact that causal relations and belief in objects are absolutely universal and belief in an intelligent designer is not, can be overcome once we realize the fact that Hume says that in order for these former beliefs to come into play, certain experiences have to be present. And they in turn, have to contain certain elements. Our experiences must contain, for example, the perception of "constant conjunction" to form the idea of cause and effect. Without the experience or perception of constant conjunction, there would be no idea of cause and effect, but with it we have the propensity, the natural instinct, to posit necessary causal relations between objects and to act on that idea. According to Tweyman, once we realize the fact that Hume says that there must be certain conditions obtaining before a natural belief comes into play, then we can see that the universality of the belief in an intelligent designer is also conditional. It is widely diffused, it is almost everywhere, because the conditions are widely diffused, but they are not everywhere. So the objection that it is not a natural belief because it is not universal, Tweyman says can be overcome by noting that Hume maintains that our impressions must contain certain elements in order for nature to give rise to a natural belief, and Hume says the same thing with regard to religious belief. Given the requisite elements, nature gives rise to the belief in an intelligent designer. The requisite elements in the case of an intelligent designer would be attention to the means/ends relations among objects. Once attention to means/ends relations takes place, nature gives rise to the belief in an intelligent designer of the relations.

But there are a number of problems with Tweyman's analysis, not the least of which is the fact that Hume never said in the *Natural History* that the belief in an intelligent designer of the universe is the only kind of belief in an invisible, intelligent power. Belief in an invisible, intelligent power could be animistic. It could also be polytheistic. Even granting that an intelligent designer of the universe is the belief which nature would suddenly give rise to once we attended to the means/ends relations among objects and parts of objects (for example in organisms), it is still unlike the non-controversial cases of natural beliefs, such as the belief in objects and the belief in causal relations between objects, in that those beliefs are both necessary for survival and shared with other animals and belief in an intelligent designer is not. Hume makes the case for this in the *Treatise* and in the *Enquiry*.[21] He never makes the case for this with regard to belief in an intelligent designer or belief in an invisible, intelligent power (the latter subsumes the former). However, there is something to the claim that Philo seems to think that the belief in an intelligent designer is natural in some sense. My suggestion is this: Hume is taking for granted the view expressed in the *Natural History of Religion,* that belief in an "invisible intelligent power" is *weakly* natural, that is to say it is widely diffused because it is based on a secondary principle of human nature which could be thwarted or inoperative for one reason or another. There could be, as Tweyman suggests, a failure to attend to means/ends relations. In that case the belief in an intelligent power would not be actualized. But attending to means/ends relations involves reasoning and attending to strong natural beliefs does not.

The belief being considered in Part XII as the belief "as some people hold," as Philo says, "that the cause or causes of order in the universe probably bear some remote analogy to human intelligence," is vague enough to allow for diverse ideas of invisible, intelligent power. Philo asks, in effect, about this belief, "What can we do when we are confronted with an argument for this but to say that it looks to be more plausible than implausible?" This formulation of Philo's statement in Part XII leaves open the possibility of many different specific conceptions. Polytheism and monotheism are obvious possibilities, but the conception of the "cause or causes of order" need not be a supernatural conception at all. The formulation that Philo gives in Part XII of the *Dialogues* also allows for the cause or causes of order in the universe to be immanent, yielding the possibility of a conception akin to pantheism as well.

Now, in various places throughout the course of the *Dialogues* Philo has suggested that we need not go beyond the universe in our speculations and that indeed we would not be warranted in doing so. If we take this stricture together with the formulation in question, this yields a kind of pantheism. This would be to say that the cause or causes of order in the universe are *immanent* and they probably bear some remote analogy to human intelligence. It is not obvious that a sophisticated pantheistic conception would require other qualities of human nature to be remotely analogous to the cause or causes of order in the universe. But it is quite clear that traditional monotheistic conceptions of deity, polytheistic conceptions, and traditional deism all attribute other qualities than intelligence to deity, qualities such as virtues and passions. These latter conceptions involve the full-fledged anthropomorphism that Hume abhors and that Philo consistently argues against throughout the *Dialogues*. The type of argument that Philo gives against anthropomorphism is an informal version of a reductio ad absurdum. This may be one more reason for thinking that pantheism is actually being privileged above these other types of god concepts, because with pantheistic concepts one would not have to go beyond the universe and one would not be required to attribute other elements that may be analogous to human personality to the deity. Whereas in traditional deistic, monotheistic, and polytheistic conceptions, virtues and passions are routinely attributed to the deity and, at least in theistic and deistic conceptions and even some among polytheistic conceptions, the deity is the creator god, necessitating our going beyond the universe in our speculations.

All these different forms of belief involving the idea of invisible, intelligent power are weakly natural for Hume. They do not have the status of belief in objects or causal relations between objects, but they are based on propensities of human nature. They are not strictly universal, nor are they necessary for survival, nor do we share them with animals. Even if it is true, as Tweyman maintains, that it takes attention to means/ends relations for this belief to be activated, then even when a belief in an invisible, intelligent power as a source of design is activated, this still leaves open possibilities for polytheism. Beyond this, the fact that it requires attention to means/ends relations among objects, and that not even all humans attend to means/ends relations, seems to strongly suggest that Hume would not think that animals possess a belief in an intelligent designer of the universe. However, animals need to survive and they need to recognize objects and causal relations between objects in order to distinguish food from foe. In Hume's view they must then possess the requisite beliefs, just as we must. But a belief in an intelligent designer is not necessary for survival, and so no species has a need to possess it, nor does Hume claim that other-than-human animals possess such a belief. Also, we may assume that Hume would hardly think that we share religious beliefs with animals, given that he did not think that all humans had these beliefs.

Given that Hume does claim that religious belief is based on principles of human nature, we may wonder whether he had some positive religious belief of his own. It is not unusual to hold that he does, however, it is not clear what positive religious views we might glean from Hume's writings. Our task is complicated by the fact that a naturalist may respond to the presence of nature with a sublime sense of awe, mystery and uplifted feelings which some may regard as intrinsically religious. If this be so, then there is a sense in which a naturalist may be "religious." I shall argue that Hume was a "religious naturalist."

A popular view of Hume is that he was an atheist. But an atheist claims that there is no divine being whatsoever. The atheist could not know this. On Hume's theory of knowledge, he would have no justification for such a claim. Hume could not claim to know that there was no God any more than he could claim to know that there was a God. On epistemic grounds, he could only have been an agnostic. And the whole discussion of the teleological argument is in terms of probabilities rather than certainties. At least, this is the tack that Philo seems to have been taking. So I think that Hume's principles, as well, perhaps, as his inclinations, would rule out atheism.

It might be said that Hume actually was a believer. Tweyman argued, in effect, that although he did not *know*, he *believed*, i.e., Hume had a theory of "natural belief" that required theism. But it seems that "non-controversial" natural beliefs, like causality, rest on "custom or habit," which is instinctual, and gives rise to beliefs that are strictly universal. Theism is not like the belief in cause and effect, which does seem universal. So, I do not think that Tweyman's discussion of *"natural belief"* can be made to be a basis for a Humean *theism*.

Hume does seem to have a "sense of religion" as Philo calls it. This sense of religion is, most likely, pre-philosophical. But the only philosophically respectable way to justify this sense, for Hume, seems to have been an argument from the "evident" instances of design in the universe. Being a philosopher, he could not help but realize all the problems inherent in such a justification, the only justification available given his empiricist principles. His principles are those of a religious skeptic, but his "sense of religion" prompts him to believe. However, his philosophical scruples will not allow any precise definition of what it is he is to believe concerning the "divine intelligence." One thing seems certain; it is not an anthropomorphic conception. Beyond that, it may be immanent or it may be transcendent. Since Philo seems not to want to go beyond the universe in his speculations, the divine intelligence may well have been regarded as immanent by Hume. For example, Philo says, "It were better...never to look beyond the present material world" (Part IV). He says this in the context of the discussion as to whether the principle of order is in the material world or in an ideal world. If it is immanent, then Hume's position is closer to pantheism than it is to either theism or deism. This would be consistent with the overall naturalism that he expresses in the *Treatise* and the *Enquiry*.

I have argued that Hume's principles require agnosticism, philosophical skepticism with regard to belief in God. Where he seems to make Philo come over to theism at the end of the *Dialogues,* this may be one last irony in a work full of ironies. It is absurd to depict God as having human passions. Revelation does depict God as having passions analogous to human passions. Therefore, a flight to revelation is a flight to absurdity. Cleanthes should take no comfort in Philo's "concessions."

Hume was not a theist. He was an agnostic whose inclinations (his "sense of religion") prompted him to belief. The "official" statement of this belief (Philo's statement) is this: "That the cause or causes of order in the universe probably bear some remote analogy to human intelligence." But the statement of his belief is consistent with deism and pantheism. I do not believe that Hume was a deist, because he did not want to go beyond the universe in his speculations. But to call Hume a pantheist seems too strong. His "official" statement of his belief (Philo's statement) is, admittedly, a "somewhat ambiguous, at least, undefined, proposition." To call Hume a pantheist might suggest that his philosophy was Spinozistic. I do not think we would be warranted in going that far. However, analogies between Hume's metaphysical position and Spinoza's "God or Nature" are important and will be discussed further in the following chapter.

It seems appropriate to call Hume a "religious naturalist." In contemplating the universe, Hume was struck with wonder at its presence, aesthetic feeling for its apparent evidences of order, horror at its unconcern for its progeny,[22] and curiosity concerning its "secret springs and principles." Its presence, for Hume, was a brute fact which presents us with "inexplicable mysteries." Its "principles" were natural laws. He fully accepted a Newtonian approach in empirical enquiry as being consistent with this naturalism,[23] but he thought that nothing could be proven about "the origin of worlds" in this way. Hume thought the subjects of cosmology and cosmogony had as their object of study something vast, sublime, magnificent, mysterious.

This view brings to mind a religious naturalist of our own time. Einstein and Hume both inquired into the general subjects of astronomy and physics in their own time and place, with all the differences in outlook that that implies. Both Einstein and Hume wondered at the universe, and about its "secret springs and principles." And they both seem to have had a similar kind of religious feeling with regard to it. Clearly, Hume was aware that "religious sentiments" are not universal. And so was Einstein, who called his religious sentiments "cosmic religious feeling." He goes on to say that it can give rise to "no anthropomorphic conception of God, and it is very difficult to elucidate."[24] For the "New Newton" it was the "most important function of art and science to awaken this feeling and keep it alive in those who are receptive to it,"[25] and as we shall see, this was true for old Hume as well.

## Chapter II

## Notes

1. Robert Hurlbutt, "The Careless Skeptic: The Pamphilian Ironies In Hume's Dialogues," *Hume Studies* 14, no. 2 (November 1988): pp. 247–248.
2. David Hume, *Dialogues Concerning Natural Religion,* ed. Henry D. Aiken (New York: Hafner Press, 1984), p. 82.
3. Ibid., p. 95.
4. Ibid., p. 39–41.
5. Ibid., p. 94.
6. This raises questions that will be treated in Chapter IV.
7. Hume, *Dialogues,* ed. Aiken, p. 34.
8. Ibid., p. 94.
9. Stanley Tweyman, *Scepticism And Belief In Hume's Dialogues Concerning Natural Religion* (Dordrecht: Martinus Nyhoff Publishers, 1986), p. 137.
10. Hurlbutt, *Hume, Newton and the Design Argument* (Lincoln: University of Nebraska Press, 1985), p. 222.
11. Hume, *Dialogues,* ed. Aiken, p. 29.
12. Ibid.
13. Hume, *The Natural History of Religion,* ed. H.E. Root (Stanford: Stanford University Press, 1956), p. 21.
14. Ibid.
15. Ibid.
16. Ibid.
17. These latter beliefs are *absolutely* universal.
18. Harris says that the whole point of the *Dialogues* is that religious belief is natural. "The 'Naturalness' of Natural Religion," *Hume Studies* 12, no. 1, (April 1987): p. 11.
19. Hume, *The Natural History,* p. 21. Emphasis added.
20. Keith Yandell, in a recent work, *Hume's Inexplicable Mystery: His Views on Religion* (Philadelphia: Temple University Press, 1990), p. 26, argues that Hume's treatment of propensities in the *Treatise* parallels his account of the genesis of religious belief in the *Natural History.* He, too, employs the distinction between "strong" and "weak" natural beliefs, and says that religious beliefs are "weakly natural" for Hume, p. 26.
21. Hume, *A Treatise of Human Nature,* ed. Selby-Bigge and P.H. Nidditch (Oxford: Oxford University Press, 1980), p. 178; *Enquiries Concerning Human Understanding and Concerning the Principles of Morals,* ed. L.A. Selby-Bigge (Oxford: Oxford University Press, 1980), p. 55.

22. The "problem of evil" presents a barrier to attributing virtues to God on the basis of an a posteriori argument such as the design argument.

23. Robert Hurlbutt, *Hume, Newton and the Design Argument*, p. 147. See also, Antony Flew, *Hume's Philosophy of Belief* (New York: Humanities Press, 1961), p. 225.

24. Albert Einstein, *Ideas and Opinions by Albert Einstein*, ed. Carl Seelig, et al (New York: Crown Publishers, 1954), p. 38.

25. Ibid.

# Chapter III

## Supernaturalism vs. "Religious Naturalism"

Within the vast literature on David Hume there is a large and significant sub-literature on Hume as a philosopher of religion. The recent works of J.C.A. Gaskin, Keith Yandell and Stanley Tweyman each make important contributions to this growing literature.[1]

It is a truism to say that each has his own "Hume." The "Humes" produced in our minds through reading, reflection and discussion are bound to differ one from another. We might think though that, after all, my Hume cannot be so radically different from yours. Our differences will be determined by our interests and emphases, not by a discernment of radically different principles in Hume. A difference in views which could justly be called "radical" is the difference between reading Hume as believing in two worlds and reading him as believing in one, i.e., reading him as a supernaturalist as opposed to reading him as a naturalist.

On some of the fairly standard themes in Hume there is much agreement on what he thought. At least we might say that commentators more or less concur on analyses of Hume's theory of impressions and ideas and his view that there is no substantial "self." But a focus on Hume's writings concerning *religion* has yielded radically different views of his commitments and projects. To paraphrase Francis Bacon, a casual acquaintance with Hume may make him an atheist to "men," but depths in Hume studies turns some people's minds toward a reappraisal of his views on religion.[2]

It is well known that Hume had a contempt for what he called "vulgar superstition" and "enthusiasm." But there are times when he seems to extol what is referred to variously as "true theism" or "true religion" or the "genuine principles of" theism or religion. Both of these themes can be found in the *Natural History of Religion*, and on the face of it, talk of true theism suggests that Hume had a positive religious belief of his own. In Sect. XV of the *Natural History* in the "General Corollary," Hume says,

"As the good, the great, the sublime, the ravishing are found imminently in the genuine principles of theism; it may be expected from the analogy of nature, that the base, the absurd, the mean the terrifying will be equally discovered in religious fictions and chimeras."[3]

Those who believe that Hume held a positive religious belief of his own do not normally take this belief to be tantamount to an acceptance of the Judeo-Christian tradition nor to any other historical religious tradition. His belief, it is variously argued, is an "attenuated" or "mitigated," or "minimal" form of deism or theism. A thin supernaturalism, usually coupled with virtuous behavior, is claimed to be the Humean "True Religion."

There is also a widely accepted approach in Hume scholarship which stresses what is referred to as Hume's "naturalism," following Norman Kemp Smith. According to this view, Hume held that human nature makes it necessary to take for granted a world of objects between which causal relations obtain. Hume sees human beings as having certain natural "propensities," some of which are irresistible and some of which are not. The former give rise to what may be called "this-worldly" beliefs and the latter give rise to "other-worldly" beliefs.

I will argue that Hume held a "naturalistic" as opposed to a "supernaturalistic" view of the world, but that the appropriate way to think of this naturalism is as a complex of metaphysical, epistemological and axiological concerns and views, viz., "religious naturalism." I call this naturalism "religious" because it encompasses both faith and doubt in certain metaphysical truths which are related to overriding ethical concerns.

Hume himself held that the existence of a world of causally related objects can be doubted in reflective moments. As a firm conviction in a metaphysical view which cannot be proven, this naturalism itself bespeaks an element of faith. Hume's "True Religion," I shall argue, is not a supernaturalism of any type, however thin. It is a faith in the "givenness" of a shared world ordered by natural laws which are, for the most part, "secret" and "inexplicable."

Hume wrote as much or more on the topic of religion as on any other single topic, with the exception of the history of England. He wrote two works specifically devoted to religion, the *Dialogues Concerning Natural Religion* and the *Natural History of Religion*. He wrote a number of essays, some of which were published as independent essays, such as "Of Superstition and Enthusiasm" and "Of the Immortality of the Soul," and some of which were incorporated into other works, e.g., the essay "Of Miracles" and the essay "Of a Particular Providence and of a Future State," which are contained as Chapters X and XI in the first *Enquiry*.[4]

To begin, one might wonder why Hume spent so much time on religious questions when, with the possible exception of the teleological argument, he thought that religious claims rested neither on putative matters of fact nor on relations of ideas. Why not simply commit works containing religious positions to the flames and have done with them? The answer is that Hume thought "traditional religion" to be pernicious, detrimental to human society, and he saw philosophy as the only antidote.

Why leave the common light of day and travel into these dark and obscure realms? Because it is here where supernaturalists take their stand:

> Chased from the open country, these robbers fly into the forest, and lie in wait to break in upon every unguarded avenue of the mind, and overwhelm it with religious fears and prejudices.

Of the different species of philosophy outlined in Sect. I of the *Enquiry*, Hume's is carried on in "the easy manner." It is not the "abstractedness of these speculations" which recommends that manner of philosophizing, but something else. Hume says,

> Happy if we can unite the boundaries of different species of philosophy, by reconciling profound inquiries with clearness, and truth with novelty! And still more happy, if, reasoning in this easy manner, we can undermine the foundations of an abstruse philosophy, which seems to have hitherto served only as a shelter to superstition, and a cover to absurdity and error![5]

What is a philosopher concerned about the well-being of humanity to do? Should the philosopher let the supernaturalists have the territory they have staked out? On the contrary, "Is it not proper to draw the opposite conclusion, and perceive the necessity of carrying the war into the most secret recesses of the enemy?"[6] Hume was at war with religion and the spoil of victory was the greater happiness of humanity.

In *Hume's Philosophy of Religion*, J.C.A. Gaskin argues that Hume is an "attenuated deist."[7] He says that "Again and again in private and in published work Hume gives explicit or implicit assent to the proposition that there is a god."[8] He quotes a number of remarks of Hume's by way of documenting this claim. There are also four "opinions" which are claimed to "follow" from Hume's "attenuated deism."[9] And there are five other opinions which, Gaskin argues, Hume "certainly held" but which, "do not follow from his attenuated deism."[10] Nevertheless, these five additional opinions seem to be regarded as corollaries to Hume's basic view, such that Gaskin concludes that Hume's overall religious position consists of "...a basic assent of the understanding to the proposition that a god exists, together with nine other items..."[11] Together they give us an "overall picture" of Hume's position as a "...highly attenuated deism which is not positively advocated."[12]

In order to characterize Hume's view as an "attenuated deism," Gaskin must hold that Hume believed at least three things: that the "cause or causes of order" actually is a single cause; that the single cause of order is transcendent to the world rather than within it; and that the single transcendent cause of order in the world created the world in which it causes the order. A further point—the remote analogy to human intelligence only probably obtains. This means that it may not obtain. But deism seems to require that it does obtain. I have found no textual evidence that Hume positively argues for any of these positions. The remarks Hume makes about God do not come as the conclusions of arguments. Gaskin also recognizes this; he says Hume's "attenuated deism" is not positively argued for.

Essential to Gaskin's position that Hume was an "attenuated deist" is the view that Hume gave assent to the proposition "that there is a god." Since I will want to examine Gaskin's position in some detail, it will be useful to have all the quotations provided by Gaskin in support of this view.

In the *Treatise,* Hume apparently does give assent to the proposition that there is a god of some kind. Gaskin cites a remark in a footnote to the Appendix of that work where Hume says, "The order of the universe proves an omnipotent mind; that is, a mind whose will is constantly attended with the obedience of every creature and being. Nothing more is requisite to give a foundation to all the articles of religion."[13]

A citation from Hume's essay "The Stoic" is one which, Gaskin admits, may be taken as representing the Stoic's point of view rather than Hume's own view. But Gaskin says that when this is taken "in company" with other remarks of Hume's, it "...seems merely to repeat what Hume says elsewhere..."[14] The quotation in question is the following: "There surely is a being who presides over the universe; and who with infinite power and wisdom, has reduced the jarring elements into just order and proportion."[15]

The third quotation provided by Gaskin in support of Hume's deism is from a letter that Hume wrote, "...in which Hume hopes that Mr. Leechman would answer an objection to: '...everything we commonly call religion, except the Practice of Morality & the Assent of the Understanding to the Proposition that God exists.'"[16]

The fourth is the well known quotation from the "Author's Introduction" to *the Natural History of Religion,* in which Hume says, "The whole frame of nature bespeaks an intelligent author; and no rational inquirer can, after serious reflection, suspend his belief a moment with regard to the primary principles of genuine Theism and Religion.[17]"

Gaskin also notes that similar remarks are made in the body of the text. One who is reading these quotations alone would probably have little hesitation in concluding that their author was a deist or a theist of a rather ordinary type.[18] But, we are dealing with no ordinary thinker, and Gaskin says, "...this is not avowal of belief in a god outlandishly defined."[19]

Hume's belief, Gaskin maintains, lies "...between deism and atheism. It is fostered by a feeling of design and given a weak rational basis by recognition that the order to be found in nature *could (not must)* be explained as the work of an ordering agent."[20]

But since it is argued in the *Dialogues* that nothing can be inferred to exist in a cause other than that which is sufficient to produce its effect, this "ordering agent" cannot be inferred to be a god of infinite attributes (wisdom, power, goodness, etc.). Hume's deism, if there be such, must be "highly attenuated." And that it cannot be a theistic belief at all is clear, since "...such an original source of order could scarcely function even as the start for a belief in a personal God exercising a moral jurisdiction, accessible to prayer, performing acts of intervention in his creation and worthy of adoration." While Gaskin seems to be right about this, a problem immediately arises when we consider that the quotation provided from "The Stoic" states that there is a god of "infinite power and wisdom." The tension in Gaskin's position mounts when we read that, "We should beware of so relying upon Hume's irony that we read an often repeated declaration as an often repeated denial..." I would suggest that we read the essay in question neither as irony nor as a statement of Hume's own position, but rather as a charitable presentation of a position which Hume does not assent to.[21]

So it is argued by Gaskin that Hume is a super-naturalist (a deist), but that his supernaturalism is quite thin ("highly attenuated"). Such a view makes it out that Hume believes that there is a *single* cause of order in the universe and that this cause of order *transcends* the universe.

Gaskin argues that four "opinions" follow from this basic position, and he also points out that there is independent evidence that Hume holds them. I will state these "implications" and comment only briefly. Rather than dispute them, I hope to put them in a different light. They are as follows:

> 1. That religious observances as such are at best worthless and at worst mischievous with the solitary exception of "virtue and good morals," which "alone could be acceptable to a perfect being."
> 2. That conventionally required religious observances are of too little real

importance to justify making an issue out of disregarding them.

3. That morally contentious issues, for example suicide, and moral distinctions in general, should not be referred to the decision of religious teaching but should be settled by reference to the needs and happiness of people.

4. That theological argument and dispute is "sophistry and illusion."[22]

None of these "opinions" seems *necessarily* to follow from Hume's supposed view that there is a single, transcendent cause of order. Neither do they follow necessarily if we add that the supposed single transcendent cause of order "probably bears some remote analogy to human intelligence."[23] No one of them are inconsistent with Gaskin's position concerning Hume, although they are consistent with other positions as well. These "opinions" would follow in a trivial sense if they were already built into a conception of "attenuated deism." But if not already built-in, I do not see how they can be strictly derived from it. Gaskin does not beg the question here. On page 223, he says,

> I shall call the 'plain philosophical assent' (*Dialogue* XII) to the existence of a god as indicated by the vestiges of the design argument, a god whose sole attribute is an intelligence which may bear some remote analogy to human intelligence 'attenuated deism.'

Since Gaskin takes the "plain philosophical assent" to the Philonic proposition in *Dialogue* XII to constitute the core of Hume's "attenuated deism," we should consider some of the possibilities left open by that proposition. To attribute an "attenuated deism" to Hume is to attribute to him a quite far-reaching metaphysical position. This is especially striking when one considers that Hume's objection to the design argument in *Dialogue* II is based on the fact that it involves inferences concerning the "two eternities" which go well beyond anything experience could possibly inform us of. It is not that Hume held no metaphysical positions at all; claims about human nature are metaphysical claims. But human experience can lend support to these claims whereas claims that go beyond the world of possible experience may derive no support from within that world at all. A metaphysical view based on evidence derived from the world of possible experience would be a tentatively held "this-worldly" or naturalistic view as opposed to an "other-worldly" or supernaturalistic one.

On the other hand, one might argue that the reason Hume devoted a work of his to the teleological argument was that he did see this argument as deriving some small support for a transcendent deity from within the world itself. Hume, on this view, allows that there is evidence of design or order in natural objects and processes and he concludes that its "cause or causes" probably bear some remote analogy to human intelligence. And thus, Gaskin holds that there is some small support for a mitigated supernaturalist position.

Even if we do accept the view that Hume held the position apparently expressed by Philo that "the cause or causes of order probably bear some remote analogy to human intelligence," it would still be going far beyond what is logically required of us if we hold that this is in fact a supernaturalistic position. And it would be going even farther to say that this position was either a deistic or a theistic one.

Let us consider some of the possibilities inherent in the Philonic proposition. First, although it is not an implication of Philo's proposition that the "cause or causes" are transcendent to the world, in both deism and theism a god creates the cosmos. The god is outside of, other than and beyond the cosmos. It is the "other-worldly" or supernatural cause of the cosmos. Even if the "cause or causes" could be determined on other grounds to be supernatural, that would still not result in a deism or a theism of even the thinnest type. Both of these supernaturalist beliefs are monistic and Philo's proposition leaves open both monistic and pluralistic possibilities. A reply might be that parsimony prevents us from characterizing Hume as a polytheist rather than a monotheist (or a deist). Philo states that, "To multiply causes without necessity is contrary to true philosophy..."[24]

There are four possibilities that can be derived from Philo's proposition: immanent/monistic, immanent/pluralistic, transcendent/monistic, transcendent/pluralistic. The principle of parsimony would require opting for the immanent/monistic possibility. The immanent/pluralistic possibility would have the virtue of not requiring us to postulate another world. But even the pluralism involved might be tidier, if the origin of order were immanent. It would not be implausible to regard the causes of order as being related by integration within a basic order-generating structural dynamic. We might think of them as related in the way that electromagnetism, gravity and the "strong" and "weak" nuclear forces may turn out to be related (or thought to be related) in a basic, order-generating structural dynamic.

The transcendent/pluralistic possibility is unlike the immanent/pluralistic possibility in at least two ways. First, on the transcendent/pluralistic possibility another world is required. Second, the plurality of causes can more easily be seen as working together in a dynamic structure on the immanentist view.

Once the causes of order are out of this world, who knows what else may be said to be plausible or implausible with regard to them? Perhaps the gods have wills of their own. The transcendent/pluralist possibility might be better employed to explain apparent conflict than apparent order. If the causes of order are regarded as natural forces, i.e., immanent causes, then we have our experience to guide us in judging what is plausible or implausible with regard to them. But, if the origin of order is thought to be supernatural, then no guidance from our experience will be forthcoming and an indefinite number of possibilities will have equal weight.

In *Dialogue* V, Philo says,

> To multiply causes without necessity is indeed contrary to true philosophy, but this principle applies not to the present case. Were one deity antecedently proved by your theory who were possessed of every attribute requisite to the production of the universe, it would be needless, I own, (though not absurd) to suppose any other deity existent. But, while it is still a question whether all these attributes are united in one subject or dispersed among several independent beings, by what phenomena in nature can we pretend to decide the controversy...In a word, Cleanthes, a man who follows your hypothesis is able, perhaps, to assert or conjecture that the universe arose from something like design; but beyond that position he cannot ascertain one single circumstance, and is left afterwards to fix every point of his theology by the utmost license of fancy and hypothesis.[25]

As far as supernaturalist possibilities go, the tidier types seem monistic. Yet, even the transcendent/monistic interpretation of the Philonic proposition must leave open a number of possibilities. For example, we cannot rule out the possibility that the god, although transcendent, did not create the cosmos but rather is co-eternal with the cosmos. Why not an Aristotelian god rather than a Thomistic one? Traditional deism is more parsimonious than traditional theism, but an Aristotelian origin of order is simpler still. No creation need be interposed between the god and the ordered world on the Aristotelian view, while this "unnecessary" complication is required on a theistic or a deistic view.

Within eighteenth century deism, as Gaskin points out, there was a range of views going from near orthodoxy to near atheism. In a note, Gaskin provides two definitions of "deism." The first, from the 1737 edition of Bayle's *Dictionary,* says of deists that they believe "...there is one God, a providence,...but (they) reject revelation, and believe no more than what natural light discovers to them." He also offers a second definition by Johnson from 1775. It says deism is "...the opinion of those that acknowledge only one God, without the reception of any revealed religion."

Gaskin comments that

> there is typically an affirmation of...a single creator god," and "...a thinly veiled denial of revelation...But...the affirmation may be affirmed, and the denial indicated, with almost every shade of emphasis from the near orthodoxy of Samuel Clarke...to the near complete avoidance of any affirmation at all by those like Collins...In Hume's case the denial of the credentials of revelation is complete and the affirmation very thin.[26]

Gaskin holds that Hume did affirm a weak version of deism. Perhaps this "attenuated deism" is a more parsimonious view than (at least some) traditional deisms. But if it is stretching things a bit to say that Hume was a supernaturalist of some type, it is an even wider stretch to characterize this supernaturalism as a type of deism. Among the several transcendent/monistic possibilities left open by a supernaturalistic interpretation of the Philonic proposition, deism requires more than such an interpretation itself requires. That the single cause of order, on the monistic view, bears some "remote analogy to human intelligence," does not necessitate the view that the god is a creator. Is the god simply the origin of order in the world, or did the god also create the world in which it produces order?

I am suggesting that the "plain philosophical assent" is not to the idea that there is a god at all. It is to the Philonic proposition itself. This appears to be what Philo intends when he says:

> If the whole of natural theology, as some people seem to maintain, resolves itself into one simple, though somewhat ambiguous, at least undefined, proposition, *That the cause or causes of order in the universe probably bear some remote analogy to human intelligence*...what can the most inquisitive, contemplative, and religious man do more than give a plain, philosophical assent *to the proposition*, as often as it occurs...?[27]

Gaskin's "overall picture" of Hume's religious views contains much that I would like to support. Neither do I want to deny that there are elements of Hume's view which are religious or which have religious connotations or analogues. I shall argue that this is indeed the case.

My own understanding of Hume's position is that he believed in the immanence of the origin of order. A point that comes out of my previous discussion of Hume's doctrine of "natural beliefs" is that he will often use the locution "Nature" when referring to the "cause or causes" of order. An example of this is where Hume claims that there is a "pre-established harmony" between the order of our impressions and the order of our ideas. In the *Enquiry*, Hume says:

> As nature has taught us the use of our limbs, without giving us the knowledge of the muscles and nerves, by which they are actuated; so she has implanted in us an instinct, which carries forward the thought in a correspondent course to that which she has established among external objects; though we are ignorant of those powers and forces, on which this regular course and succession of objects totally depends.[28]

Hume never gives a precise definition of "nature," but, with regard to the question of whether the origin of order is immanent or transcendent, Hume's citations of "Nature's" "determinations" make plausible the view that his position was that whatever the "cause or causes" actually are, the origin of order is immanent within the world and not transcendent to it. If this were not the case and Hume thought the origin of order was transcendent, then should we not expect many more locutions like "God" or "the gods" to denote such an origin?

Gaskin's caution that we beware of so relying on Hume's irony that we take an often repeated affirmation as an often repeated denial is a good one. The danger is that our preconceptions will guide us more than Hume's "irony" and that we will too easily "read things into" Hume that he did not hold and "read out" beliefs that he did hold. Gaskin thinks that we might make the latter mistake with regard to Hume's "attenuated deism".

When we consider how often Hume uses "Nature" to denote the origin of instincts, passions and propensities of various kinds, then I think we must say that Hume locates the origin of order within the world much more often than he locates it outside. In other words, Hume's avowal of a belief in "Nature" is actually fairly commonplace in his writing and his avowal of belief "that there is a god" is not. It is rather surprising to find any apparent avowals of supernaturalism in Hume, while the former avowals are so commonplace that a casual acquaintance with Hume can well make him seem an atheist to "men." I would suggest that too emphatic a focus on the latter "avowal(s)" could be misleading. It could lead us to attach too little significance to Hume's usual avowal of belief in immanent causation and too much to unargued remarks which seem to make him a supernaturalist.

It might be said in reply that Philo's proposition does come as the conclusion of the long argument which constitutes the *Dialogues*. While characterizing Hume as an "attenuated deist" on this basis does not impose upon him an "outlandish" position, it does require us to infer a lot more than the Philonic proposition implies, since that proposition does not necessarily imply two worlds.

To see Hume as coming to a supernaturalist position after a long argument that results in the Philonic proposition that the "cause or causes of order in the universe probably bear some remote analogy to human intelligence" is to see it as the result of philosophical thinking. Gaskin says:

> This position is that a vestigial design argument establishes a weak probability that natural order originates in the activity of something with intelligence remotely analogous to our own. This feeble *rational* datum is united with an insistent *feeling* in most of us that natural order springs from a designer. When our philosophical assent to the existence of this designer has been given (that is to say our assent qualified by the exercise of mitigated skepticism) we recognize that it has no moral claim upon us, nor we upon it. I call this position "attenuated deism."[29]

I believe this position has clear advantages as a supernaturalist view of Hume over the contrasting position of Tweyman, Harris and Hurlbutt, which is that Hume held that the supernaturalist belief in an "intelligent designer of the universe" is determined by "Nature," in accordance with his doctrine of "natural beliefs." The non-controversial cases of "natural beliefs," e.g., belief in an objective world and belief in causal relations, do not come as the conclusions of arguments. "Nature" determines that we hold them because they are necessary to our survival within it. Rather than resulting in them, philosophical argument undermines them by raising skeptical doubts.

Gaskin's view does not imply that supernaturalism is "strongly natural." "The insistent feeling in most of us" that is united to the weak "rational datum" of the design argument is not claimed to be in all of us and it is not claimed to be irresistible. But Tweyman must hold that, for Hume, "supernaturalistic feeling" is universal, irresistible and that no "rational datum" is united to it. "Nature" simply requires us to believe in its own supernatural origin.

Both views would close off possibilities that the "Philonic proposition" leaves open. This fact is perhaps more pertinent to Gaskin's view, however, since Gaskin takes "attenuated deism" to be the final position Hume arrives at, at least in part, by way of concluding an argument. If we characterize the Philonic proposition as an avowal of supernaturalist belief, then we have arbitrarily closed off possibilities left open by it. This arbitrariness seems to undermine the rationality of the "rational datum" that Gaskin sees Hume as offering in support of supernaturalism.[30]

One consideration which lends support to the view that Hume was a deist is that the "design argument" was a favorite of eighteenth century deists and it is the only argument Hume dignifies by giving a lengthy philosophical treatment. But this can be understood apart from a deist conviction on Hume's part. If we examine some of the apparent "avowals" cited by Gaskin, we can see that they have in common with Hume's naturalistic avowals (his attributions of causes to "Nature") an assumption of order or design. Hume says the *"whole frame of nature* bespeaks an intelligent author" in the "Author's Introduction" to the *Natural History of Religion*. In "The Stoic" he talks about a "being" who has "reduced the jarring elements into just order and proportion."[31] The *Natural History* quotation does not require the author of nature's "frame" to be a Creator and the quotation from "The Stoic" suggests the possibility of a Platonic Demiurge, but they both presuppose order or "design." And in the *Dialogues*, Philo seems unconcerned with the *creation* of the universe. His aim is to inquire into the origin of order in the universe and not into the origin of the universe itself. As Greg Moses has put it, "Philo is interested only in the cause or causes of order in the universe; the question of existence, or why there is anything rather than nothing, is apparently not an issue for him."[32]

What Hume shared with supernaturalists, particularly deists, is the conviction that *there is order*. This conviction in Hume can be seen as having a status approaching faith and this can contribute to a misunderstanding as to the content of Humean faith.

For Hume, it is determined by "Nature" that we believe that causal relations obtain within it. Philosophical reflection can cast doubt on the conviction that these relations obtain, but it can not eradicate it. That "Nature" is a cosmos is basic to Hume's overall philosophical position. When we consider why Hume held this conviction we learn that, ultimately, "Nature" causes him to hold it, since it is composed of two beliefs (in objects and in causal relations) that are necessary to our survival within it. It is true that skeptical doubts can momentarily undermine it, but, as Jose Maia Neto says, "...Hume mitigates the opposition (between reason and natural instinct) so that a compromise between the dogmatic input of nature and the Pyrrhonian one of reason becomes possible..."[33]

This, as I see it, is not a theoretical compromise. It is a rejection of "excessive skepticism" in favor of beliefs which an agent requires in order to survive in the world. "The great subverter of Pyrrhonism or the excessive principles of scepticism is action, employment, and the occupations of common life."[34]

I have argued previously that Hume regards the beliefs in the "self," in a world of objects or an objective world, and in causality as "strong natural" beliefs. They arise from the constitution of "human nature" and they are not successfully resisted for any sustained period. These beliefs form part of a complex of views, metaphysical, epistemological and moral or ethical, which I call "religious naturalism." Put together, the "dogmatic" metaphysical content of this faith comes to this: there is a "self" which shares a world of objects with other "selves" and that world is an orderly whole, a cosmos. Hume's naturalistic faith is in the givenness of a shared world of objects between which causal relations obtain.

Although the term "Nature" is never defined precisely, it is not importing too much into Hume to say that whenever he attributes causes to "Nature" he has reference to what he takes to be our "shared cosmos" and it is within that cosmos that the origin of order is located. But a problem immediately arises. Hume understood his belief in "Nature" to result from the functioning within "himself" (his imagination, his consciousness, his subjective experience) of the very object of his belief. He thought that the workings of "Nature" within oneself gave rise to one's belief in "Nature's" objective operations. There seems to be a circularity in this position which can contribute to skeptical doubt. As an argument, either for the existence of "Nature" or for the existence of "natural beliefs," it would be begging the question. But Hume does not give an argument here. He asserts a this-worldly faith which he thinks respects common life but which cannot be demonstrated to be true.

It is a consequence of Hume's epistemological position that the belief in the existence of an objective world of causal relations cannot be known to be true. Once skeptical doubts arise, experience can only mitigate them for an agent who must act in the world, but experience can never completely eradicate them. Nevertheless, Hume's faith is such that he trusts in the object of his faith, "Nature," more than he trusts in the deliverance of his reason. In *An Enquiry Concerning Human Understanding,* Hume talks about causal inferences in which "we infer like effects from like causes and vice versa" and says that these inferences could not be trusted to the "fallacious deductions of our reason," but rather "It is more conformable to the ordinary wisdom of nature to secure so necessary an act of mind, by some instinct or mechanical tendency...." Hume also writes, "It seems evident that men are carried, by a natural instinct or prepossession, to repose *faith* in their senses; and without any reasoning, or even almost before the use of reason, we always suppose an external universe, which depends not on our perception, but would exist, though we and every sensible creature were absent or annihilate."[35]

Pyrrhonism, or "the excessive principles of skepticism" may raise doubts, but "Nature is always too strong for principle."[36] Hume's mitigated skepticism can be seen as a compromise between faith and doubt which has analogues in theological traditions. In Hume's overall approach, his metaphysical faith in a shared cosmos and his doubt concerning that very postulate go hand in hand. Just as faith and doubt are partners on the supernaturalist's path, Hume's epistemological skepticism and his metaphysical faith both have place in his own "religious naturalism."[37]

In order to see Hume as a thin supernaturalist, we must think that his own preferred way of closing off the possibilities inherent in the "somewhat ambiguous" Philonic proposition was in favor of a transcendent/monistic explanation of the origin of order. As Gaskin says, Philo's proposition allows that order "could (not must)" be explained in such a way. The view that this was not Hume's own preference gets some support from within the *Dialogues,* i.e., this is clearly not Philo's own preference. This is unambiguously stated in Part IV, where Philo objects to what he sees as an infinite regress set up by affirming the transcendent/monistic possibility. If the origin of order requires an explanation, then opting for the view that the origin of order is a supernatural being with a design in mind would require us to explain the origin of the design that that being had in mind. Ultimately, we are left without an explanation whether we pursue the infinite regress or decide to cut it off by simply stopping it at an "intelligent designer."

Philo says of the deist's preferred way of closing off the metaphysical possibilities,

> An ideal system, arranged of itself, without a precedent design, is not a whit more explicable than a material one which attains its order in a like manner; nor is there any more difficulty in the latter supposition than in the former.[38]

Philo prefers the more parsimonious view,

> It were better, therefore, never to look beyond the present material world. By supposing it to contain the principle of its order within itself, we really assert it to be God; and the sooner we arrive at that Divine Being, so much the better.[39]

In this passage, Philo states his own immanentist preference quite clearly *and* he licenses religious talk about nature or the "present" world.

On the view that Hume was a "religious naturalist," both the "rational datum" which forms the basis for the deist's transcendent/monistic inference from the Philonic proposition and Hume's praise of True Religion can be accommodated along with Hume's attribution of a "dogmatic force" to nature. With regard to the "rational datum" of the Philonic proposition, Hume stops short of accusing all supernaturalists of complete irrationality.

He holds that an "attenuated deism" offers a possible, relatively parsimonious explanation of order or design in the world. After all, explanation must stop somewhere. As long as one's supernaturalism does not engender "religious fears and prejudices," Hume can tolerate it. His own skepticism would seem to require this toleration, since Hume cannot claim to know that supernaturalism is false.

In the absence of conclusive negative evidence, the transcendent/monistic possibility of "attenuated deism" receives some rational support from the design argument. There is design in the world and one's preference with regard to the Philonic proposition may lead one to the conclusion that a transcendent agent created it. This conclusion is not necessary, but neither is it without any reasonable basis. The basis, for Hume, is what he regards as the fact that the universe is a cosmos.

Greg Moses, in his very interesting article, "Hume's Playful Metaphysics," says that Philo's position regarding his proposition concerning the origin of order is that it is, "The only position required of all reasonable people," it being "...the minimum requirement of natural good sense..."[40] Beyond this, whichever of the various possibilities one might opt for will depend on other factors, such as, "habit, caprice, inclination, and the influence of education."[41] The deist's view, if it is attenuated, is not completely unreasonable. But it is also clear to Moses what Philo's preference is. Philo, Moses says, "...does express and argue for some personal preferences..."[42] Philo would prefer a system of cosmology which would, "...ascribe an eternal, inherent principle of order to the world, with God as this present material world supposed as containing its principle of order within itself."[43] The continuing value of Hume's "playful" foray into metaphysics in the *Dialogues* is that this kind of reflection and consideration of arguments and possibilities may check the progress of various unreflective and harmful superstitions.[44] This view of the matter is right in line with Hume's stated intention, in the *Enquiry*, of carrying the war against superstition "into the most secret recesses of the enemy."

On my view, Philo/Hume allows that there may be a very thin form of supernaturalism that is neither unreasonable nor harmful. This is what we should expect from Hume. He allows that reasonable people may prefer an option which differs from that of his own. Hume himself is not an "attenuated deist," but a reasonable person might be.

After discussing such factors as "economy," "preferences" and "instincts," Moses says,

> It is factors like these...which cause Philo to be a naturalist/material-ist/*whatever the right word is*, though acknowledging that one could be some

kind of Cleanthes-like theist, and claiming a naturalism flexible enough to be adapted to what he regards as the minimum demands of good sense in respect of the presence of design in the universe.[45]

Philo does not come over to a supernaturalist position in Part XII, and Hume's many (indeed commonplace) attributions of causation to nature support the view that neither was such a position Hume's own.

Moses points out that Philo prefers to think that there is an "eternal, inherent principle of order to the world." Moses does not quite know what to call this position. But that the universe is an orderly whole, a cosmos, and that the cosmos *itself* is an eternal reality (though reasonable people may disagree) are basic components of what I am calling Hume's religious naturalism.

The basic metaphysical component of this religious naturalism, as I read Hume, is a faith in the "givenness" of a shared world ordered by natural laws which are, for the most part, "secret" and "inexplicable." Hume considered the origin of order to be immanent. As such, it is "nature" and not a supernatural being which may bear some remote analogy to human intelligence.

"Nature" eternally, inexplicably manifests an orderly presence. On this view the "insistent feeling of design" on Hume's part, recognized by Gaskin, can be seen as a cosmic one rather than a supra-cosmic one. It is a feeling for or about the universe at large whose order permeates the very processes of our thought.

In the *Enquiry,* Hume says that nature has

> ...implanted in us an instinct, which carries forward the thought in a correspondent course to that which she has established among external objects; though we are ignorant of those powers and forces, on which this regular course and succession of objects totally depends.[46]

Nature's powers and forces, the cause or causes of order, are secret and inexplicable to us. The cosmos is ultimately mysterious.

Hume's sense of the present mystery and design of the universe, his notion that "Nature's" eternal, inherent principal of order may bear "some remote analogy to human intelligence," and what must have been a sense of beauty in the perception of the cosmos are all elements of his religious naturalism. In the second *Enquiry,* Hume says, "It is on the proportion, relation and position of parts that all natural beauty depends...(but) beauty is not in any of the parts...(it) results from the whole, when that complicated figure is as presented to an intelligent mind, susceptible to those finer sensations."[47] These same elements come together in a striking way in a clear statement of an immanentist religious position analogous to the one which I am arguing was Hume's own. The statement was made by Albert Einstein in an essay entitled "The World As I See It:"

> The most beautiful experience we can have is the mysterious....A knowledge of the existence of something we cannot penetrate, our perceptions of the profoundest and the most radiant beauty, which only in their most primitive forms are accessible to our minds—it is this knowledge and this emotion which constitute true religiosity; in this sense, and in this alone, I am a deeply religious man...I am satisfied with the mystery of the eternity of life and with the awareness and glimpse of the marvelous structure of the existing world, together with the devoted striving to comprehend a portion, be it ever so tiny, of the Reason that manifests itself in nature.[48]

Hume's religious naturalism could be expressed in a very similar way. I cite the Einstein passage to highlight how a faith in design or the "marvelous structure" of the universe, a sense of mystery in the contemplation of it, and an aesthetic response to it can come together in a self-professed religious position which is immanentist or "naturalistic" as opposed to transcendentalist or "supernaturalistic." There is even, in Einstein's use of the metaphor of "Reason," an indication that the origin of order manifested in the design of nature is regarded as bearing some remote analogy to human intelligence.

Hume is more skeptical than Einstein. Hume thought that we could not comprehend the ultimate causes of order nor did he think we could prove that the origin of order was immanent, though this was his preferred view. Philo/ Hume will only allow that a "somewhat ambiguous" and "undefined" proposition issues from a rational consideration of order or design. I have discussed the ambiguity between four metaphysical possibilities inherent in the Philonic proposition, and that the "remote analogy" to intelligence cannot be precisely defined is made clear by Philo in Part XII. Einstein has no hesitation in using the metaphor of "Reason."

Hume is more diffident than Einstein, but his "insistent feeling" of design, his sense of mystery expressed in talk of "nature's" "secret springs and principles" and what must have been his aesthetic response to the presence of the "cosmos" may all be seen as moving together in the direction of Einstein's "true religiosity" (and Hume's True Theism or True Religion). Just as Hume's epistemological skepticism is mitigated by his doctrine of "strong natural beliefs," his metaphysical faith in a natural cosmos is mitigated by his skeptical doubt. Einstein gives voice to unmitigated faith. For Hume, faith and doubt each have their say.

Hume argues against our being able to demonstrate the truth of the complex belief that Einstein presupposes, i.e., that there exists an objective world in which necessary causal relations obtain. Hume holds that this complex belief, compounded of the belief in an objective world and the belief in causality, cannot be known to be true by reasoning or experience. It can be doubted in reflective moments "in one's study." But that Hume's mitigated faith is substantially similar to an immanentist religiosity like that of Einstein is indicated by the fact that Hume thought that "nature" did not leave it to us to come to a belief in objective causal relations as a result of reflection, because it is of "too great importance" for our survival. "Nature" itself determines that we believe in its objective operations. This metaphysical belief, made necessary by the operations of that which we believe in, is one of the central tenets of Hume's overall position. It is not a thin supernaturalism, but a straightforward naturalism that provides the (metaphysical) content of Hume's faith, albeit a faith tempered by doubt.

On my view, we can see Hume as denying the dichotomy between the natural and the supernatural worlds. Collapsing the distinction results in a monistic view which is yet religious. This "present world" contains within itself its own eternal, inherent principle of order. This order pervades the course of natural events and the internal processes of thought. It is in this light, I am urging, that we should understand the following:

> ...I allow that the order and frame of the universe, when accurately examined, affords such an argument...which might immediately lead the mind to the pure principle of theism, and make it overleap, at one bound, the vast interval which is interposed between the human and the divine nature.[49]

I have argued that Hume affirms only the possibility that a reasonable person may prefer the transcendent/monistic option opened up by assent to the Philonic proposition that "the cause or causes of order in the universe probably bear some remote analogy to human intelligence." A version of this option might be to say that an intelligent creator designed the universe. An affirmation of this with regard to the deity, and nothing more, is an affirmation of the thin supernaturalism aptly termed "attenuated deism" by Gaskin. I have also argued that Hume did not himself prefer the transcendent/monistic option in any version. Rather his own preference involves a this-worldly faith in the presence of a natural cosmos: "the whole system, or united fabric of the universe."[50] It is a faith, tempered by epistemic doubt, in our participation in a shared world ordered by natural laws.

Human nature, for Hume, is a product of "nature" itself. Hume sees "nature" as eternal and as manifesting an orderly presence both within the environing universe and within the processes of thought. In *this* way, Hume's own religious naturalism "overleaps" the boundary between the human and the divine. This suggests that Hume's "true religion" is immanentist: closer to Einstein's "true religiosity" or Spinoza's "God or Nature" than to any form of a two-world hypothesis.

The "remote analogy to human intelligence" that the origin of order may bear is the element of the Philonic proposition which seems most easily to lend itself to a misreading of Hume's talk of "design" as a faith in an otherworldly designer. Penelhum quotes the Philonic proposition and says "It amounts to an admission that men are unable to refrain from ascribing some degree of teleology to the cause or causes..." But he also thinks that by this proposition "Hume seems to be committed to the existence of a vague universal deism..."[51] But we have seen how readily the metaphor of "Reason" can be used to refer to the origin of order by one who has a self-professed immanentist religious position. And I would suggest that Hume's occasional anthropomorphic talk about "nature" ("Conformable" to her "ordinary wisdom...she has implanted in us an instinct...")[52] expresses the possibility of something remotely analogous to intelligence in the "cause or causes of order" equally well. It is of some interest to pursue the possibility that Hume had some direct influence on the way in which Einstein expresses his own position in natural philosophy. Hume's biographer, Ernest Mossner, relates in the Introduction to his edition of Hume's *Treatise,* that, "Albert Einstein's biographer states flatly that 'the philosopher whose views Einstein felt helped him the most was David Hume.'"[53]

Hume undermines the theological distinction between the human and the divine, or nature and the deity, in another way as well. This comes toward the end of the first half of Part XII, before the Philonic proposition is formulated as such, where Philo "himself" argues that a merely "verbal dispute" is involved concerning the question of theism versus atheism.[54] From a consideration of "the very nature of language and ideas," Philo argues that neither the degree, nor the range of the analogies that the "cause or causes" of order may bear to observable operations of nature can be precisely determined.[55] Any number of operations may bear a certain degree of analogy.

As to the degree of the analogy to human intelligence, Philo says the "theist" will allow that the difference between the divine mind and the human mind is "great and immeasurable" and the "atheist" will allow that operations of nature such as the "rotting of a turnip, the generation of an animal, and the structure of human thought" are remotely analogous to each other[56]. And, since there is no precision to be had here, the atheist would also agree that it is probable that the "principle" of order also bears "some remote inconceivable analogy to the other operations of nature and, among the rest, to the economy of human mind and thought."[57]

The dispute between theists and atheists is one concerning the degree of analogy between only one of the operations of "nature," i.e., the processes of intelligent thought, and, in any case, disputes of this nature do not admit of a precisely determined resolution. Although Philo asserts that there probably is an analogy, it is the implications of a "plain philosophical assent" to the proposition that lead into verbal disputes;

> The theist allows that the original intelligence is very different from human reason; and the atheist allows that the original principle of order bears some remote analogy to it.[58]

The theist and the atheist may even "insensibly change sides" with regard to an emphasis on the *degree* of analogy.[59] The theist may "exaggerate the dissimilarity" between the "original intelligence" and the human in order to magnify the greatness of his god compared to "frail...mortal creatures," and the atheist might press the strength of the analogy, *extending* it to "all the operations of nature."[60] I think the thrust of my argument so far makes it plausible to read these remarks as a caution from Philo/Hume. The caution is precisely *not* to take the Philonic proposition, about to be formulated a few pages forward in Part XII, as being an expression of supernaturalism on the basis of the "remote analogy" itself.

I suggest that the "verbal dispute" passage is better understood if we see Hume himself as a naturalist. For the naturalist to say that the "principles of order" may bear a remote analogy to intelligence on the one hand and to say that the "wisdom" of "nature" is very different from our own on the other *is* to enter into a dispute as to the strength of an *analogy*. But if the dispute is about whether there is one world or two, then the dispute is metaphysical and not merely "verbal."

In considering Hume's "final position" on the design argument, Nelson Pike comments on the relationship between the "verbal dispute" and the "remote analogy" of the Philonic proposition:

> ...Philo argues that the traditional debate between the atheist and the theist has been largely a dispute about words and not about matters of substance. If he

is honest, Philo says, even the atheist must admit that the "operations of nature" bear at least a "remote analogy" to one another and to the operations of artifacts. In turn, this requires that the atheist admit at least a "remote analogy" between the cause of the universe and human intelligence.[61]

Pike disambiguates that "ambiguous and undefined" proposition in favor of a certain version of the transcendent/monistic option opened by it, i.e., that an intelligent creator designed the universe. He points out that Philo has previously said that it is "evident" "that the works of nature bear a great analogy to the productions of art."[62] He then suggests that we have here a way of understanding "the sentence in Philo's last speech in which the cause of the universe is described as bearing only a "remote analogy" to human intelligence."[63] He sees in "Philo's last speech" a straightforward endorsement of the argument from design. Considering the "plain philosophical assent" to the Philonic proposition, Pike says, "As I read this speech, the point is wholly affirmative as regards the conclusion of the argument from design."[64] Pike sees Hume as emerging "in the end as the champion of Natural Theology."[65] In order to deny this, Pike says, "Philo's apparent endorsement of the argument from design in Part XII is to be interpreted as something other that what it appears to be."[66]

I have quoted Philo giving what I think is a plain rejection of the transcendent option, in favor, on the basis of parsimony, of his own preferred option which is an immanentist one. The way in which Pike refers to the "sentence" in "Philo's last speech" is such that it is already interpreted as referring to a *single cause* of *the universe* as probably bearing a remote analogy to human intelligence. I believe this to be an instance of an understandable misreading of Hume's "insistent feeling of design" as a faith in a supernatural creator/designer. That the remote analogy is to intelligence may seem to license a transcendent reading, because of the suggestion of a teleological element or quality in the "cause or causes of order in the universe." And since polytheism is probably not a live option for Hume, it is easier to see a "vague" or "attenuated" deism as being Hume's option of choice.

The "plain philosophical assent" is to the Philonic proposition itself, I have argued, and not to any particular version of any one of the four metaphysical possibilities opened up by it. Pike does not quote the "sentence" in full. The proposition that "men of reason" must give a "plain philosophical assent" to is: "That the cause or causes of order in the universe probably bear some remote analogy to human intelligence." Pike, Gaskin and Penelhum all seem to close off the possibilities in favor of a certain version of the transcendent/monistic option, the creator/designer version.

I have advanced several reasons for not reading the Philonic proposition in this way. Apart from the fact that Hume's many criticisms of religion make it seem antecedently implausible that he himself was a supernaturalist:

1) The creator/designer version of the transcendent/monistic possibility opened up by the Philonic proposition is not identical to that proposition itself, but is to the proposition itself that a "plain philosophical assent" is given. The proposition itself allows for Philo's own immanentist preference.

2) Philo prefers the immanentist option, it being the more parsimonious one.

3) Hume regularly imputes causation to "nature," and so he regularly locates the origin of order within this "present world."

4) The (remote) analogy to intelligence can be accommodated by a religious position that does not postulate two worlds (Einstein), and Hume's talk about "nature's" "ordinary wisdom" can accommodate it just as well.

I have attempted to refute the view that Hume was what I call a "thin supernaturalist" and to show that, for Hume, True Religion was immanentist and therefore this-worldly and naturalist. That his naturalism required faith, and that this faith required its object, has a certain circularity, of which Hume was, I think, well aware.

This understanding of Hume's position can accommodate his extolling of "true religion," while at the same time dispensing with the "inconveniences" of attributing a supernaturalist position to him. It can accommodate the former, in part, by recognizing the self-conscious element of faith in Hume's metaphysical view, and by attentively considering the expressions of wonder, mystery, and what appears to be a kind of religious and/or aesthetic emotion in the *Dialogues:* Hume's "insistent feeling of design." This is expressed as a sense of the sublimity of the *cosmos* even in the midst of skeptical doubt. These expressions of wonder, mystery and so forth, are consistent with Hume's skepticism, which can be seen as mitigated with regard to experience, but unmitigated with regard to what is, in principle, beyond all possible experience.

In Hume's religious naturalism, his epistemological skepticism and his metaphysical naturalism go hand in hand. It is a consequence of Hume's epistemological position that the existence of an objective world of causal relations cannot be demonstrated. Once doubts arise, experience can only mitigate, but never completely eradicate them. However, Hume's metaphysical naturalism is such that he trusts in the object of his belief, "nature," more than he trusts in the "fallacious deductions of our reason."

Hume's true religion is not a supernaturalism of any type, however thin. It is a robust naturalism which provides the content of Hume's faith. His belief is in the "givenness" of a shared world ordered by natural laws which are, for the most part, secret and inexplicable. It is an achievement of the Great Skeptic to see that a position which holds that we live, and move, and have our being in a shared cosmos, a view eloquently expressed by Einstein and widely pre-supposed in other quarters, is as much an article of faith as are any of its possible alternatives.

## Chapter III

## Notes

1. J.C.A. Gaskin *Hume's Philosophy of Religion,* Humanities Press, Int. (New Jersey: Atlantic Highlands, 1988); Stanley Tweyman, *Scepticism And Belief In Hume's Dialogues Concerning Natural Religion* (Dordrecht: Martinus Nyhoff Publishers, 1986); Keith Yandell, *Hume's Inexplicable Mystery: His Views on Religion* (Philadelphia: Temple University Press, 1990).

2. David Hume, *The Natural History of Religion,* ed. H. E. Root (Stanford: Stanford University Press, 1956). Hume quotes Francis Bacon on page 42, "A little philosophy, says Lord Bacon, makes men atheists; A great deal reconciles them to religion." He explains by saying that when "superstitious prejudice" leads theists to "lay stress on a wrong place"; and they then discover "by a little reflection" that nature is orderly "their whole faith totters and falls to ruins"; but then they discover "by more reflection, that this very regularity and uniformity is the strongest proof of design and of a supreme intelligence." We know from Hume's treatment of the design *argument* in the *Dialogues* and by the similar treatment in the *Enquiry,* Sect. XI, that he did not think "the strongest proof" was all too strong. But that it is the "strongest proof" available is due to its appeal to the order which is observed, for example in "constant conjunctions" between certain events.

3. *Natural History,* "General Corollary."

4. Ten of Hume's various writings on religion have been gathered together recently, edited by Anthony Flew, *David Hume: Writings on Religion* (La Salle, Illinois: Open Court Publishing, 1992).

5. David Hume, *Enquiries Concerning the Human Understanding and Concerning the Principles of Morals,* Second Edition, ed. L. A. Selby-Bigge, (Oxford: Oxford University Press, 1980), p. 11.

6. Ibid., p. 12.

7. J.C.A. Gaskin, *Hume's Philosophy of Religion,* pp. 219–29.

8. Ibid., p. 219. Gaskin's emphasis.
9. Ibid., p. 223.
10. Ibid.
11. Ibid., p. 229.
12. Ibid.
13. Ibid. Gaskin is quoting from Hume's *Treatise,* ed. Selby-Bigge, p. 633.
14. Ibid.
15. Ibid.
16. Ibid., p. 219
17. Ibid.
18. Ordinarily, deists and theists believe that there exists an all-good and all-powerful god who created the universe. The major difference being that theists believe that this god works miracles in history, can be influenced by prayer, etc., and deists do not believe in supernatural interventions of any kind. Deists believe that the god made the universe to run on the natural laws he created for it, without interference.
19. Ibid., p. 220. If we consider theism outlandish, then Gaskin is surely right about this. Whatever else one might make of Hume's discussion of miracles in the *Enquiry,* one cannot get a *belief* in miracles out of it. It follows that there can be no divine revelation nor intervention in response to prayer for Hume, these both being miracles.
20. Ibid., p. 221. Emphasis added.
21. Ibid., p. 220. Compare this to Hume's essay, "The Platonist," where he gives eloquent voice to a Neo-Platonic metaphysical position.
22. Ibid., p. 222.
23. David Hume, *Dialogues Concerning Natural Religion,* Part XII, ed. Aiken, (New York: Hafner Press, 1984), p. 94. Philo is speaking. I shall call Philo's statement that "the cause or causes of order in the universe probably bear some remote analogy to human intelligence" the Philonic proposition.
24. Ibid., p. 40.
25. Ibid.
26. Gaskin, op. cit., p. 244.
27. David Hume, *Dialogues,* ed. Aiken, p. 94.
28. David Hume, *An Enquiry Concerning Human Understanding,* p. 55.
29. Gaskin, op. cit., pp. 6–7.
30. Stanley Tweyman, *Scepticism And Belief In Hume's Dialogues Concerning Natural Religion.* Tweyman avoids this problem at the expense of seeming to make Hume a fideist, that is, Hume would hold that we must believe in a Creator because the creator framed our nature such that the belief is irresistible. Hume does say this kind of thing about beliefs that "nature" causes us to hold, but faith in design should be distinguished from faith in a transcendent designer. Hume never says that "nature" causes us to hold the latter belief.
31. Hume also says, in "The Stoic," that the being did this with "infinite power and goodness," but this is a position Philo consistently rejects in the *Dialogues* and Hume offers no argument for it in his writings on religion.

32. Greg Moses, "Hume's Playful Metaphysics," *Hume Studies* 18, no. 1 (April, 1992): p. 71.

33. Jose R. Maia Neto, "Hume and Pascal: Pyrrhonism vs. Nature," *Hume Studies* 17, no. 1 (April 1991): p. 46.

34. Hume, *Enquiry*, p. 159.

35. *An Enquiry Concerning Human Understanding*, pp. 55 and 155, emphasis added.

36. Ibid., pp. 158 and 150.

37. In a work entitled *On the Boundary*, Paul Tillich gives a personal statement of his own position which may well have come from David Hume. Tillich says, "At almost every point, I have had to stand between two alternative possibilities of existence, to be completely at home in neither and to take no definitive stand against either. Since thinking presupposes receptiveness to new possibilities, this position is fruitful for thought; but it is difficult and dangerous in life, which again and again demands decisions and thus the exclusion of alternatives. This disposition and its tension have determined both my destiny and my work." Quoted by Thomas Indinopolous in *The Erosion of Faith* (Chicago: Quadrangle Books, 1971), p. 90.

38. Hume, *Dialogues*, ed. Aiken, p. 36.

39. Ibid., p. 34.

40. Moses, op. cit., p. 66.

41. Ibid., p. 68.

42. Ibid., p. 65.

43. Ibid.

44. Ibid., p. 70.

45. Ibid., p. 68.

46. Hume, *Enquiry*, Sect. V, Part II, p. 55.

47. Hume, *An Enquiry Concerning the Principles of Morals*, Appendix I, p. 291–92. Examples of aesthetic response to the design in nature can be found in various places in the *Dialogues*. They are voiced by different speakers, for example in Part II, Cleanthes speaks of the "minute parts" of nature as having an "accuracy" which "ravishes into admiration" all who contemplate them. And Philo, in Part V, speaks of the "immense grandeur and magnificence of the works of nature" revealed by astronomy (*Dialogues*, ed. Aiken, pp. 17 and 37).

48. Albert Einstein, "The World As I See It," *Ideas and Opinions by Albert Einstein*, ed. Carl Seelig et al (New York: Crown Publishers, 1954), p. 11.

49. Hume, *Natural History*, p. 24. Although I have transposed the order of two sentences, the sense of them remains the same. But for the fact that Hume is skeptical of all metaphysical postulates, even his own, we might think that his view that "nature" itself is the eternal or "divine" reality coincides with that of Spinoza. For other analogies between Hume and Spinoza, see Wim Klever's "Hume Contra Spinoza?" in *Hume* Studies 16, no. 2 (November, 1990) and subsequent discussions. The present analogy is one between (what I am arguing is) Hume's religious naturalism and Spinoza's "God or Nature."

50. Ibid., p. 25.

51. Terence Penelhum, "Hume's Skepticism and the Dialogues," *McGill Hume Studies*, ed., David Fate Norton et al (San Diego: Austin Hill Press, 1979), pp. 274–75. I have argued that the Philonic proposition does reflect Hume's own faith in order/design, but that the proposition itself is not tantamount to the transcendent/monistic option it opens up.

52. Hume, *Enquiry*, p. 55.

53. *A Treatise of Human Nature*, ed. Ernest Mossner (London: Penguin Books, 1969), p. 27. There is much evidence of the influence of Hume on Einstein. One need only read Einstein's essay on Bertrand Russell's philosophy, "Remarks on Bertrand Russell's Theory of Knowledge," in *Ideas and Opinions by Albert Einstein*, where Einstein spends most of his time praising Hume. Alan Lightman's book, *Great Ideas In Physics* (New York: McGraw-Hill, 1992), pp. 158-60, contains a section entitled, "Deductive versus Inductive Thinking and the Influence of Hume on Einstein." I'd like to thank David A. Gangursky for bringing Lightman's book to my attention.

54. Hume, *Dialogues*, ed. Aiken, p. 85.

55. Ibid.

56. Ibid., pp. 85–86.

57. Ibid., p. 86.

58. Ibid.

59. Ibid.

60. Ibid.

61. Hume, *Dialogues Concerning Natural Religion*, ed. Nelson Pike (Indianapolis: Bobbs-Merrill Co., 1970), p. 216.

62. Ibid., p. 218. I read this as no more, nor less than one among other expressions of an aesthetic response to "nature" in the *Dialogues*.

63. Ibid. The "sentence" referred to is the italicized sentence near the end of Part XII which I have been calling the Philonic proposition.

64. Ibid., pp. 218–19.

65. Ibid., p. 208.

66. Ibid.

# Chapter IV

# "Religious Naturalism" and Miracles

Hume's much discussed essay, "Of Miracles," in Section X of *An Enquiry Concerning Human Understanding,* displays his faith in immanent and thus "natural" causation more clearly than any of his other writings on religious topics. His naturalistic presuppositions are employed toward the end of carrying on the war against superstition into the "secret recesses of the enemy." For it is clear at the outset that Hume thinks that belief in miracles is mere superstition. He believes he has discovered an argument which,

> ...if just, will, with the wise and learned, be an everlasting check to all kinds of superstitious delusion, and consequently, will be useful as long as the world endures. For so long, I presume, will the accounts of miracles and prodigies be found in all history, sacred and profane.[1]

As a superstition, a belief in miracles is without any rational foundation, for Hume. Its genesis lies in ignorance coupled with various emotions of a negative kind. In his essay, "Of Superstition and Enthusiasm," Hume says that, "Weakness, fear, melancholy, together with ignorance, are...the true sources of superstition."[2] Throughout his essay on miracles, Hume opposes his own faith in a natural cosmos to what he takes to be a "pernicious corruption" of "true religion."[3] To put a check on superstition would be to check the bigoted persecutions of others and the harmful and unnecessary fears and anxieties in ourselves with which superstitions are associated. This is one of Hume's general purposes in the *Enquiry,* as he expresses it in the opening section.[4]

The more particular purpose of the essay "Of Miracles" is to undermine belief in the founding miracle of Christianity, i.e., the physical resurrection of Jesus Christ from the grave. In various subtle and not so subtle ways Hume opposes his own faith in a natural cosmos to the supernaturalism of Christianity. Towards the end of Part II of his essay, Hume concludes that,

"...we may establish it as a maxim, that no human testimony can have such force as to prove a miracle, and make it a just foundation for any such system of religion."[5] Christianity is such a system,[6] but this is not necessarily true of all religions.

Hume's own religious naturalism, his faith in a shared cosmos as a system of inviolable natural laws, intrudes upon his argument in such a way as to leave him open to charges of question-begging by critics. Others maintain that Hume's arguments against the credibility of the Gospel testimony to the Resurrection are successful.[7]

In this chapter, I will consider the kinds of arguments Hume gave on the question of miracles, with a particular focus on the founding miracle of Christianity. I will try to show that Hume gave varying kinds of arguments with different results, all the while opposing his own faith to "pernicious superstition."

Hume approaches the question of miracles from two different but overlapping perspectives, as a natural philosopher and as an historian. In the first case, he is concerned with the possibility and/or probability of the occurrence of miracles. This is controversial and speaks to the issue of whether Hume begs the question against miracles. In the second case, he expresses an historian's concern for the proper assessment of testimony to the occurrence of a miracle. He gives several arguments from both perspectives. And he always presupposes his metaphysical naturalism from either perspective, with varying consequences for his arguments.[8]

I shall argue that there are four possible arguments that can be identified in the essay "Of Miracles," each with different, but overlapping aims:[9]

*Impossibility*  The first argument is the, possibly, a priori argument against the possibility of miracles. This is the argument, or possible argument, which gives rise to charges of question-begging. The view that this first argument is a question-begging one is controversial and runs counter to the interpretation of the argument by Flew and others.[10] I will discuss Flew's interpretation and some objections and replies after having explained my position on the Impossibility argument. I shall argue that Hume held that the requirements of a "miracle's" occurrence make it an incoherent notion because they lead to contradictions; that this argument is based upon his metaphysical presupposition of uniformities or constant conjunctions but that it is effective against the claim that a "miracle" as a "violation of a law of nature" is a meaningful notion. If one shares Hume's assumption that the universe is an orderly whole, a cosmos, such that a "common course of nature" obtains, and one claims that a miracle occurred, then Hume shows the overwhelming difficulties in making that miracle-claim a coherent one. We will see that Hume's adversaries on this point have traditionally shared his assumption. But the Impossibility argument is inapplicable outside of the framework of a view of the universe as a cosmos. Within that framework, we see Hume's own faith pitted against the supernaturalism of Christianity.

*Implausibility* The second argument is that against the plausibility of accepting testimony as evidence for the occurrence of a miracle. Here Hume considers the value of documentary testimony as evidence from an historical perspective. I shall argue that Hume's criteria for evaluating testimony are cogent and that an application to the Gospel testimony undermines the plausibility of the testimony.

*Improbability* The third is an argument against the strong probability of the occurrence of miracles. The conclusion of this argument is that the probability of the occurrence of miracles, such as it is, should be judged to be very weak. The support for the Improbability argument and the Indistinguishability argument, to follow, overlap somewhat in that some of the supporting statements offered for one conclusion will also be relevant to the other.

*Indistinguishability* The fourth argument that can be derived from Hume's essay on miracles is against the possibility of distinguishing miracles from anomalies, based on empirical evidence alone. I argue that this fourth argument is successful and, a fortiori, we must accept the conclusion of the second argument.

The Indistinguishability argument is a conceptually based argument but it is not against the possibility of miracles. It is against the possibility, for any given extraordinary phenomenon, that empirical evidence could verify the alleged fact that it *is* a miracle rather than merely a presently unexplainable natural event. This is an argument which leaves open the theoretical possibility of miracles, but it renders them less harmful from a Humean anti-superstitious perspective, since it renders them less capable of functioning as the foundation of a religion.

The second argument, the Implausibility argument, is independent of the fourth, the Indistinguishability argument, but if the fourth is successful, as I believe it is, then the second argument is successful for even stronger reasons. This is because mere historical documentation of reports of a miracle, as Hume argues, has never provided a sufficient basis for believing that one actually occurred. In support of this, Hume provides criteria for assessing historical documents which contain testimony to the occurrence of miracles. His targets here are religions which appeal to literary traditions containing reports of miracles which are then taken to be those religions' instituting and justifying or validating phenomena such as Christianity offers.

My aims are to identify and clarify Hume's several concerns and arguments in his essay, "Of Miracles" in Section X of the first *Enquiry* and to show how these have place in the developing theme of Hume's own "religious naturalism."[11]

Hume begins his essay "Of Miracles" by informing the reader that he intends to promulgate an argument "of a like nature" to "...Dr. Tillotson's...against the *real presence*..."[12] Tillotson, the theologian and prelate, had been appointed Archbishop of Canterbury in 1691 and he had given an argument against the Catholic doctrine of "transubstantiation."[13] According to this scholastic doctrine, the host or wafer used in the performance of a Mass becomes transformed, in its metaphysical substance, into the body of the God, Jesus Christ, while its accidents remain the same. The wafer is transformed into the flesh of Christ while still looking, feeling and tasting like a wafer to the senses.

Tillotson argued that if "Transubstantiation be part of the Christian Doctrine, it must have the same confirmation with the whole, and that is Miracles."[14] For Tillotson, the founding miracles of Christianity, as reported in the New Testament writings, have the testimony of "eyewitnesses" in support of them. The evidence available to the "eyewitnesses" is the direct evidence of their senses. So, ultimately, the "confirming" miracles of "Christian Doctrine" rest on the foundation of sensation. Accordingly, the Catholic doctrine of Transubstantiation cannot be part of "Christian Doctrine," "...For a man cannot believe a Miracle without relying upon sense, nor transubstantiation without renouncing it."[15] For all that the evidence of the senses can tell us, no change takes place in the wafer. Consequently, transubstantiation cannot be proved by a miracle, "...because that would be, to prove to a Man by something that he sees, that he does not see what he sees."[16]

If a miracle were wrought in proof of the doctrine of transubstantiation, then two things would have to obtain: first, knowledge of its occurrence must rest on the certainty of sensation; secondly, the "proof" it affords would require us to renounce what the senses certainly seem to tell us regarding the lack of change in the wafer. Such a "proof" would "draw several ways," as Tillotson has it.[17] It would require us to both affirm and deny the "certainty" of sensory evidence. Tillotson concludes his argument by saying that "...the main Evidence of the Christian Doctrine, which is Miracles, is resolved in the certainty of sense, but this Evidence is clear and point-blank against Transubstantiation."[18]

Hume paraphrases Tillotson's argument and in doing so he highlights something Tillotson is perhaps aware of, but that he passes over rather too lightly in his argument. It is that for us, and excepting that the truth be "brought home to everyone's breast, by the immediate operation of the Holy Spirit,"[19] the evidence of the Christian Doctrine can only be "resolved into the certainty of sense"[20] indirectly, by accepting the testimony of the Apostles that they had first-hand experience of the foundational miracles of Christianity. The appropriate conclusion, which Hume draws, and which Tillotson passes over, is,

> Our evidence, then for the truth of the *Christian* religion is less than the evidence for the truth of our senses; because, even in the first authors of our religion, it was no greater; and it is evident it must diminish in passing from them to their disciples; nor can anyone rest such confidence in their testimony, as in the immediate object of his senses.[21]

With this, Hume sets the stage for his own argument, "of a like nature" to Tillotson's but which has the aim of putting "...an everlasting check to all kinds of superstitious delusion."[22]

In Part II, Hume does not try to oppose sensory evidence against sensory evidence, as Tillotson had attempted to do, in order to undermine belief in Transubstantiation. Hume opposes sensory evidence to *testimony to the occurrence of a miracle* in order to undermine belief, based on testimony, in all miracles whatsoever, and particularly belief in *the* putative foundational miracle of Christianity—the Resurrection.

Hume begins by reiterating his empiricist view that "experience be our only guide in reasoning concerning matter of fact."[23] But experience also informs us of the uncertainty of itself as a guide, "...by that contrariety of events, which we may learn from a diligent observation."[24] While some events have been found to have been constantly conjoined "in all countries and all ages," others have been variable and less than constant in their conjunction with each other.[25] This means that in our reasonings concerning matters of fact there are varying degrees of assurance that we may have with regard to them, "...from the highest certainty to the lowest species of moral evidence."[26]

So, Hume begins by laying the groundwork for an argument similar to Tillotson's. Experience is our only guide concerning matters of fact, but this guide is not infallible: "All effects follow not with like certainty from their supposed causes."[27] Some events have been found to have been constantly conjoined, but others are more variable. Empirical reasoning can involve various degrees of probability. Hume seems to identify "degrees of assurance" with "probability," so that one may say that this is a "subjective" conception of probability. It is the judgement of the likelihood of an event that the "wise man" will make, upon weighing the evidence. If events have been constantly conjoined, then the "wise man" who "proportions his belief to the evidence" regards the empirical evidence as a "full proof" of the future existence of such a conjunction.[28] In other cases, where events are more variable, we must weigh "opposite experiments."[29] We must consider "which side is supported by the greater number."[30] Here we do not have a "proof," but rather, "the evidence exceeds not what we properly call *probability.*"[31]

Hume then applies these principles to the particular instance of testimony evidence, "the reports of eyewitnesses and spectators."[32] He says that he will not dispute "about a word," if one should deny that arguments based on testimony rely on the relation of cause and effect.[33] But he makes the point, the only point he needs to make, that with regard to all objects there is no "discoverable connexion" between them, and the testimony of eyewitnesses is not an exception to this maxim. The connection of testimony with the truth of what is testified to "seems as little necessary as any other" connection between one species of "object" and another.[34] Hume says:

> ...as the evidence, derived from witnesses and human testimony, is founded on past experience, so it varies with the experience, and is regarded as either a proof or a probability, according as the conjunction between any particular kind of report and any kind of object has been found to be constant or variable.[35]

The perception of "constant conjunction" in all times and places is not something anyone can have experience of and is part of Hume's naturalistic faith or religious naturalism. We live in a shared cosmos. It has a history and we who share it can reflect on and are affected by its history. Hume the skeptic is notorious for arguing that none of this can be certainly known, but as a philosophical historian, a natural philosopher and "always a man," he took it all for granted.

With regard to testimony from "eyewitnesses," Hume the historian is concerned to lay down what may be regarded as "informal" but useful criteria for its evaluation. There are several factors in eyewitness testimony which can constitute a "contrariety" in the evidence. Testimony can be opposed by "contrary testimony," or contrariety of evidence can result from the character of the witnesses, or their number; from their manner of testifying, or from a "union of all these circumstances," since:

We entertain a suspicion concerning any matter of fact, when the witnesses contradict each other; when they are but few, or of a doubtful character; when they have an interest in what they affirm; when they deliver their testimony with hesitation, or on the contrary, with too violent asseverations.[36]

In Part II of the essay "Of Miracles" Hume applies these criteria to the miracles reported in the Bible and, I shall argue, succeeds in producing a non-question-begging argument which seriously undermines the credibility of the testimony.

In Part I Hume allows, for the sake of argument, that the testimony of "eyewitnesses" to a miracle "...considered apart and in itself, amounts to an entire proof."[37] Now, a miracle is a violation of the "laws of nature" brought about by God or some "invisible agent."[38] On the other hand, a "law of nature" is indicated in the constant conjunctions between events which afford us a "proof." That these conceptions result in certain tensions is a major theme in all of Hume's arguments.

I now turn to Hume's four possible arguments concerning miracles. The Impossibility argument overlaps the Indistinguishability argument. The Impossibility argument is against the possibility of miracles. The Indistinguishability argument is against the possibility of distinguishing miracles from anomalies. The Indistinguishability argument allows for the possibility of miracles, but says that if a miracle occurred, it could not be identified as such on the basis of empirical evidence alone.

Hume has been criticized because he does not say precisely what his conception is of a "law of nature." David Fate Norton provides Hume with a plausible candidate for a "law" by focusing on the role of constant conjunctions in "proofs." Since constant conjunctions are uniform past experiences, the formulation of a law of nature, Norton maintains, can be for Hume, "...no more, strictly speaking, than a summation of a wholly uniform past experience."[39] But it does seem that Hume has more than summations of constant conjunctions in mind when discussing "nature's" laws. As we have seen, these laws are "secret" and "inexplicable," whereas a summation of constant conjunctions can only be made on the basis of accumulated observable experiences. Moreover, Hume makes an implicit distinction between constant conjunctions and "laws of nature." A question is whether Hume thinks that constant conjunctions are both necessary and sufficient for a law, the law being simply a summation of uniformity, or whether constant conjunctions are necessary but not sufficient for a law. If the latter, then Hume need only maintain that where there is no constant conjunction there is no law. I shall argue that the latter position is Hume's own position.

If one thinks that Hume requires a clear conception of a law which states necessary and sufficient conditions for that law, then a "summation of a wholly uniform past experience" may provide what is required. This conception of a Humean "law of nature" does seem to get some support from the text. Hume says:

> A miracle is a violation of the laws of nature; and *as a firm and unalterable experience has established these laws,* the proof against a miracle, from the very nature of the fact, is entire as any argument from experience can possibly be imagined.[40]

A "firm and unalterable" past experience has "established" these laws, so it is not implausible to think that a summary statement of a uniform past experience would just *be* what a law is.

If Hume had wanted to offer a "law" then all he could have offered is, as Norton says, a "summation" of uniform past experience. Though Hume did not offer any "laws," he had a belief in their existence. The implicit distinction Hume makes between constant conjunctions and laws of nature comes in the sentence after the one just cited:

> Why is it more than probable, that all men must die; that lead cannot, of itself, remain suspended in the air; that fire consumes wood, and is extinguished by water; unless it be, that these events are *found agreeable to* the laws of nature...[41]

Constant conjunctions, such as fire consuming wood, would not be "more than probable," if they were not agreeable to the "laws of nature." But a summary statement of a uniformity, e.g., (under the appropriate circumstances) "fire always consumes wood," is not itself the law. If the statement "fire always consumes wood" is true, then it is because it is "agreeable" to a law. The constant conjunction and the law to which it conforms are distinct. That "fire always consumes wood" is not a statement of the necessary and sufficient conditions of the constant conjunction between the wood's being on fire and its being consumed. "Laws of nature" are more than or other than summary statements of simple uniformities (constant conjunctions).

Hume says that, "nothing is esteemed a miracle, if it ever happen in the common course of nature."[42] But the "powers and forces" by which the "course of nature" is governed are "wholly unknown to us."[43] In Hume's religious naturalism, the "laws of nature" are mysterious metaphysical ultimates governing the orderly succession of events. And these laws, the "cause or causes of order," are beyond the ken of human intelligence, although they may bear some remote analogy to it.[44]

It is true, as critics have maintained, that Hume cannot give an account of a law of nature. But it is not true that this fact constitutes a weakness in his discussion of miracles. Hume needs only to state a necessary condition which, if violated, would show that there was no law underlying a particular conjunction of events. A necessary condition of a law's underlying (underwriting, grounding) a particular conjunction of events is that the conjunction be experienced as uniform or constant. And this is precisely what Hume provides when he says, "There must, therefore, be a uniform experience against every miraculous event, otherwise the event would not merit that appellation."[45] Since an event must violate a law of nature in order to be miraculous, it must constitute a break in the constancy or uniformity of certain conjunctions in order to merit the name, otherwise we couldn't know that it actually violated a law. If it is "in the common course," then it is not "esteemed a miracle."

Hume had not claimed to be able to provide a clear statement of a "law of nature." Indeed, he claimed that no one could provide this. The laws, as metaphysical ultimates, are wholly unknown to us. But the "common course of nature" is given in our experience of various uniformities. Were there no uniformities, there would be no "common course of nature." But if there were no "common course" there would be no laws. Thus, uniformities are necessary for laws. Hume need not say that the uniformities themselves constitute the laws in order to say that uniformities must be violated for an event to be "esteemed" miraculous.

We may now state the analogy with Tillotson's argument in the following way: miracles require that there be a law of nature which obtains in order to be violated *and* that there be no law, since the break in constant conjunctions means that no law in fact obtains. If there is a law of nature that requires a constant conjunction which can be summarized as "the dead remain dead," then there can be no physical resurrections. But if there is a physical resurrection, then there can be no law of nature that obtains which requires that the "dead remain dead." Any evidence in support of a putative "law of nature" obtaining will at the same time be evidence against the possible violation of that law. Conversely, any evidence in support of a putative violation of a law will at the same time be evidence against the possibility of that law obtaining. The conclusion is that belief in miracles fares no better than the Catholic doctrine of Transubstantiation, since the latter doctrine "draws several ways" and, in a like manner, so does the former.

Tillotson had argued that if the wafer undergoes a change of substance, then we cannot trust our senses. But the evidence for Christianity, miracles, as reported by "eyewitnesses" who gave their testimony, would then be undermined. It would be undermined because that evidence is based on the sensory observation of the miracles reported. And if we could not trust our senses, then the evidence would be suspect. Tillotson concludes that Transubstantiation can be "no part of Christian Doctrine." Likewise, according to Hume's arguments, as I interpret them, it is crucial that miracles require that there be a violated law, since this provides tensions which "draw several ways."

Given the foregoing account of Hume's argument in Part I, there are two possible conclusions that may be drawn. The first is the Impossibility conclusion. Since miracles require a law and they themselves constitute a violation of or a break in constant conjunctions, they require that there both be and not be the requisite law. Thus, miracles are impossible because the very notion of a miracle is incoherent. It is internally contradictory. While miracles may be part of "Christian Doctrine," they can be no part of intelligible discourse simply because they require a violated law. And thus, the miraculous physical Resurrection of Jesus Christ from the grave is impossible because it requires a law that is not a law.

The other conclusion that may be drawn from my account of Hume's argument in Part I is the Indistinguishability conclusion. It assumes a "miracle" is a coherent notion, therefore, miracles are possible. Consider the following: Since the Resurrection would have constituted a break in the conjunction between dying and remaining dead and ex hypothesi the testimony to the Resurrection amounts to a "full proof," we have prima facie evidence that the statement "the dead remain dead" is not underwritten by a law of nature. At first sight, this would mean that the Resurrection is a total anomaly. It would be, at least at present, a completely unexplainable event. But the possibility of its being explained in natural terms in the future cannot be ruled out. If it was a miracle, then we would already have an explanation to hand. It was God, violating the laws of nature in order to raise Jesus Christ from the grave and to prove the truth of "Christian Doctrine." This is precisely where the problem lies.

According to the Indistinguishability argument, if we have a "full proof" that the dead have not always remained dead, then it is plausible to think that there is no law of nature which underwrites a summary statement of a constant conjunction such that "the dead remain dead." The empirical evidence alone, in this case the testimony of "eyewitnesses" based on sensory observation, cannot insure that the event was in fact a miracle rather than a presently unexplainable natural event, i.e., an anomaly.

If we have proof that Jesus rose from the grave, does that mean that there is a God of the appropriate kind and that God violated a natural law in order to make Jesus rise? Or does that mean that we have misconstrued nature's laws? Evidence of the Resurrection alone would be insufficient to distinguish it as a miracle rather than an anomaly.

The point can be generalized: for any given extraordinary, putatively miraculous event, strong empirical evidence that it did indeed take place would be sufficient to raise the question of whether the laws of nature have been violated or whether we have misconstrued the laws. But the evidence would not be sufficient to answer this question.

> Thus, suppose, all authors, in all languages, agree, that, from the first of January 1600, there was a total darkness over the whole earth for eight days: suppose that the tradition of this extraordinary event is still strong and lively among the people: that all travellers, who return from foreign countries, bring us accounts of the same tradition, without the least variation or contradiction; it is evident, that our present philosophers, instead of doubting the fact, ought to receive it as certain, and ought to search for the causes whence it might be derived.[46]

If we were convinced that the event took place, it would always be reasonable to seek its natural causes. The conclusion of the Indistinguishability argument is that, for any given extraordinary event, empirical evidence alone can never be sufficient to distinguish it as a miracle rather than an anomaly.

Although Hume does not precisely spell out the "like nature" of his argument to Tillotson's argument, both the Impossibility argument and the Indistinguishability argument display an important analogy to Tillotson's view that the doctrine of Transubstantiation "draws several ways." The Impossibility argument maintains that a belief in miracles "draws several ways," because it maintains that belief in a miracle requires both that there be and not be the requisite *violated law*. The Indistinguishability argument "draws several ways" because it maintains that an extraordinary, putatively miraculous event would always make it reasonable to question whether there was or was not a violated law and the answer to *this* question would not be forthcoming based only on the evidence of the event's having taken place.

So far I have argued that Part I of Hume's essay "Of Miracles" contains two separate arguments against belief in miracles. The first argument, which I have termed the Impossibility argument, maintains that the requirements of a miracle's having taken place are contradictory, since a miracle requires both that there be and not be a uniform past experience in order to occur.

As I understand the Impossibility argument, Hume states it succinctly as follows:

> A miracle is a violation of the laws of nature; and as a firm and unalterable experience has established these laws, the proof against a miracle, *from the very nature of the fact,* is as entire as any argument from experience can possibly be imagined.[47]

A miracle requires that we have evidence of a constant conjunction which is not uniform. That is why, "from the very nature of the fact," the Impossibility argument is as strong as can be imagined. I am in general agreement here with Antony Flew when he says,

> ...there cannot but be a conflict, even a contradiction, within any suitably comprehensive case for saying that a miracle has actually occurred. Such a case has to show first, that the supposed laws, of which the actual occurrence of the putatively miraculous events would constitute an overriding, do in fact obtain, and second, that the overridings have actually occurred.[48]

Hume was so assured in his judgment of the physical possibilities relevant to certain miracle claims that he goes so far as to say, "that a dead man should come to life...has never been observed in any age or country."[49] And this leads to the charge of question-begging, to which I now turn.

In his essay, "Hume on Miracles: Begging-The-Question Against Believers," Benjamin F. Armstrong, Jr. says,

> The begging-the-question charge against Hume is straight-forward: To argue that the reports of the Resurrection are to be dismissed on the grounds that the event conflicts with a law of nature, if the law depends on the assumption that resurrections have not occurred, is to assume what one is to demonstrate in order to demonstrate it.[50]

Now, I have claimed that one can distinguish four different arguments in the essay "Of Miracles." They can be distinguished by their conclusions, although their supporting statements may overlap and they can be put together in various ways. Support relevant to one conclusion will also be relevant to another. All the arguments have the same purpose, which is to undermine belief in miracles.

I have discussed the Indistinguishability argument and I have discussed the Impossibility argument. After having considered objections and replies to the "begging-the-question charge," I shall discuss the Implausibility of the notion that testimony to the occurrence of a miracle could make that miracle a "just foundation" upon which to found a religion. I maintain that all four conclusions are given or endorsed by Hume for the reasons he gives in the essay.

Armstrong, however, follows a number of commentators in referring to "Hume's argument."[51] The version Armstrong gives has elements of what I call the Impossibility argument, although the Implausibility conclusion can receive support from it as well. Armstrong says,

> According to the popular understanding of Hume's argument in Section X of the *Enquiry*, the laws of nature are to be deployed to rule out events that miracle-reporters report (the Resurrection, for example). The support for the occurrence of the allegedly miraculous event is the testimony of the miracle-reporter along with whatever support is available for the reporters reliability. On the side of the law(s) of nature is a 'firm and unalterable experience' understood to be the completely regular course of events that supports the law(s). The one-sidedness in favor of the law(s) of nature is so great that the law(s) is (are), far and away, epistemically preferable to the report of the reporter. Hence the occurrence of the event is ruled out and the testimony rejected.[52]

Armstrong allows that there would be a "conceptual conflict between the description 'law of nature' and the description 'violation of a/that law' of nature,"[53] but his first move is to withdraw the latter description from the Resurrection. He says,

> ...the conflict so generated is a conflict between a proposition *under the description* 'law of nature' and an event *under the description* 'violation of a law of nature.' Hence the conflict that is generated creates, at most, a problem for *describing* the event reported as a violation of a law of nature. No such conflict is generated by the description "resurrection." So, no conflict is generated/presupposed by claiming that a resurrection has occurred.[54]

Simply to claim that a resurrection has occurred is not necessarily to make the further claim that the occurrence violated a law of nature. There would be no conflict between describing a law and describing a violation of a law, if there were no claim that a particular event constituted a violation of a law. As Armstrong sees it, this puts the burden of proof on Hume. He says, "As a consequence, if Hume's argument is to rule out resurrections (which it does, as Hume sees it),[55] not just rule out calling resurrections 'violations of laws of nature,' non-question-begging support is required of a law of nature, 'the dead remain dead.'"[56]

Now, it does seem clear that Hume wants to undermine belief in the Resurrection. His invented case of the resurrection of Queen Elizabeth seems transparent on this point.[57] And to undermine the foundational miracle of Christianity would be to undermine "all kinds of superstitious delusion(s)" which are associated with it. But can Hume actually "rule out" the Resurrection? If it is claimed that the Resurrection was a miraculous intervention by God into the orderly course of nature, then I think he can, because such a claim generates his Impossibility argument. However, if that claim is withdrawn and the incoherent notion of a "miracle" is not employed, then there seems to be no impossibility in the case and a resurrection could have occurred, although it still may seem implausible to believe so based only upon the testimony to its occurrence.

If the burden of proof is successfully shifted to Hume, then I think that he cannot bear up under the strain. Armstrong puts the question-begging charge (where the resurrection is *not* claimed to be a "miracle") in the following way:

> A Humean assessment of the resurrection-reporter's claim would then require support for a law of nature, 'the dead remain dead.' But this is precisely where the risk of begging questions is encountered. Support for such a law is to be sought in, among other things, the historical record, which includes reports of resurrections as well as 'reports' of the dead remaining dead.[58]

Where there is no claim that an event is a "miracle," there is no incoherence in trying to establish its possibility. So, there is no incoherence in the simple claim that a dead man came back to life where that claim is not coupled with the further claim that the event was miraculous. Hume could not "rule it out." The Impossibility argument relies on the idea, which Armstrong also accepts, that there would be a "conceptual conflict" in the notion of a violated law of nature.[59] *No "miracle" claim, no conceptual conflict.* There may have been a non-"miraculous" resurrection. While this may still seem implausible, the Impossibility argument cannot "rule out" such an event. If there is another sense of the term "miracle" that is coherent and that does not presuppose an orderly succession of events, none is offered in Armstrong's essay.

So a contemporary "believer," such as Armstrong may be, is free to believe that the reports of the Resurrection contained in the New Testament writings are not claims that an impossible event took place, i.e., a traditional "miracle." But what price freedom? The Humean succeeds in undermining

Christianity either way. Either the miraculous physical Resurrection of Jesus Christ from the grave is impossible because the notion of a miracle is incoherent, or the resurrection of Jesus possibly did occur but it was not a miracle as traditionally understood. If one rejects the former alternative and affirms the latter, then the Resurrection (resurrection) can no longer perform the role it formerly played in the history of Christianity. That role had been to provide the proof that the Christian religion was instituted by God. As Tillotson and all the orthodox have always maintained, "...the main Evidence of the Christian Doctrine...is Miracles."[60] Armstrong, of course, sees that his problem is to get the notion of a miracle back together with the reports of the Resurrection, and he ceases to use the word "miracle" in favor of the phrase "act of God."

Armstrong had argued that if Hume or a Humean wanted to "rule out" reports of a resurrection as being false, then evidence would be necessary to the effect that there is a law of nature such that "the dead remain dead." But part of the evidence of what the "common course of nature" had been in the past would be historical documents. These documents contain reports of the dead not having always remained dead. If we failed to treat these reports as evidence, then we would have begged the question against the reporters. If we did accept the "resurrection-reporter's" reports as evidence, then we could not have sufficient support for a law of nature such that "the dead remain dead." The Humean must either beg the question, or allow that a (non-miraculous) resurrection is possible.

Armstrong believes that withdrawing the description "violation of a law of nature" from the resurrection (Resurrection) does more work than simply allowing the possibility of a non-miraculous resurrection taking place. This is just his first move in pressing the "begging-the-question charge." He says,

> As Hume's argument is popularly understood, it presents a case against the occurrence of resurrections. Clearly to rule out a resurrection is to rule out the act of God the resurrection was to be. But to block the case against the occurrence of a resurrection, as a successful charge of begging-the-question does, is to destroy Hume's particular case against the occurrence of an act of God, for Hume's case against an act of God is nothing more than his case against a resurrection.[61]

For reasons already stated, the last clause of the last sentence of the above passage is simply incorrect. Hume's case against the "act of God" that the Resurrection was to be is the Impossibility argument, which maintains that the notion of a miracle is incoherent, given the further assumption that a miracle is an act of God which is contrary to the "common course of nature." Unless an "act of God" is not to be considered a "miracle," it is successful against the claim that the *Resurrection* occurred. If it is not considered to be a "miracle" in the sense used in Hume's essay, then we either need another sense of the term or a criterion to distinguish "acts of God" from other events.

To "block the case" against the occurrence of a (non-miraculous) resurrection with a successful charge of begging the question is one thing, but to claim that this is also effective against the position that the notion of a traditional miracle is incoherent is quite another claim. Armstrong does hold to the traditional understanding of a "miracle," but he thinks that Hume has no longer any case to make against the notion.

If it is claimed that the Resurrection was to be an "act of God" as this has been traditionally understood, then the burden of proof is shifted back to the miracle-reporter. Traditionally, an act of God has been thought to be identifiable, at least in part, by a suspension of the "common course of nature" of which that act is supposed to be the cause. We will see that Armstrong shares this traditional view. It will not do to show that a resurrection is possible. It must also be shown that the notion of a "miracle" is a coherent notion, so that the Resurrection may also be an "act of God" (and play its traditional role in Christianity). But an attempt to show that the Resurrection could have been an "act of God" runs afoul of Hume's Impossibility argument when that act is claimed to violate a "common course of nature."

The conclusion of the present discussion is that Hume, in order to "rule out" resurrections, would have to show that they are impossible and this he cannot do, for a number of reasons. But it is sufficient to argue, as Armstrong does argue, that Hume cannot claim to know that the dead coming to life "has never been observed in any age or country" in the face of reports to the contrary. However, if someone claimed, as Armstrong does claim, that the Resurrection "was to be an act of God," i.e., a "miracle," then the burden is on the miracle-claimer to show that the notion of a miracle is an intelligible notion. And this he cannot do. The charge that Hume begs-the-question against resurrections is successful but a charge that he begs-the-question against miracles is not. Hume had read Campbell's "Dissertation on Miracles," in which the question-begging charge was initially raised. But as far as I can tell from a letter Hume wrote to the Rev. Hugh Blair (probably circa 1761) he seems unconcerned with the charge. This may well be because his argument is directed against belief in miracles, not against non-miraculous events, however extraordinary. He writes to Blair, "Does a man of sense run after every silly tale of witches or hobgoblins or fairies, and canvass particularly the evidence? I never knew any one, that examined and deliberated about nonsense who did not believe it before the end of his enquiries."[62]

Suppose an "act of God" is not thought to be a "miracle." The claim would simply be that the Resurrection occurred as an "act of God." In an indeterministic universe there would be no constant conjunctions and no Humean "laws of nature," i.e., there would be no laws which underwrite the conjunctions.[63] Can Hume "rule out" an "act of God" that is not claimed to be a "violation of the laws of nature?" It seems not. In the context of Hume's view of "nature" as a cosmos, "acts of God" in history would be "miracles," as they were for Tillotson and as they have been regarded in the main historical tradition.

Thomas Aquinas had said that, "those things are properly called miracles which are done by divine agency beyond the order commonly observed in nature."[64]

In the orthodox tradition, when God acts in history either to resurrect or reveal, it is an act which goes beyond, overrules, suspends or modifies "the common course of nature." Generally, the-act-of-God-claimer makes the further claim that there is a "common course of nature" which God suspends. However, the act-of-God-claimer does not need to make this further claim. The contemporary believer might claim that since the universe seems to be indeterministic, we can dispense with the idea of uniformities in the conjunction of events. The "conceptual conflict" between a proposition *under the description* 'law of nature' and an event *under the description* 'violation of a law of nature'" may be dissolved by dispensing with *both* of these descriptions. In an indeterministic universe the dead can be raised and information can be revealed by God without such a "conceptual conflict." Surprising dis-conjunctions of events otherwise commonly conjoined can occur spontaneously.

Hume's argument is inapplicable to an "act of God" which is thought of as a violation of the common course of nature where the "common course" *does not* entail exceptionless uniformities in the conjunction of any events. "Uniformities," however, help clarify what is meant by a "common course of nature." The notion is exceedingly vague without this clarification.

The believer either holds that the universe is indeterministic or he does not. If he does not, then Hume's Impossibility argument applies. If he does, then the way seems closed to being able to distinguish an "act of God" from any other event. All events could be "acts of God" in an indeterministic universe, but then there would be no special evidence of the truth of

"Christian Doctrine." Unless some coherent criterion can be employed to distinguish events which are "acts of God" from events not to be so described, the believer would still have a problem answering a suitably modified Humean Indistinguishability argument.

I have been concentrating on Hume's discussion in Part I of the essay "Of Miracles." I believe Armstrong puts together arguments in Part I and arguments in Part II which should be kept distinct. Armstrong says that, "If Hume's argument fails to challenge the epistemic status of the testimony that a resurrection has occurred, the epistemic status of that testimony is not jeopardized by the reporter's (additional) claim that the event is a violation of a law of nature."[65]

The "epistemic status" of the testimony is not challenged because Hume cannot "rule out" the possibility of a resurrection in the face of reports to the contrary. Hume does jeopardize the "(additional) claim" that a violation of a law of nature occurred with the Impossibility argument. In Part II of Hume's essay he also challenges the credibility of testimony to the occurrence of a "miracle" by introducing considerations which challenge the credibility of the reporters and waiving problems in establishing a miracle's possibility.

In Part I, Hume had allowed that the testimony to a "miracle" could possibly amount to an entire proof. The challenge was to clarify what that claim could mean. But in Part II, Hume says,

> In the foregoing we have supposed, that the testimony, upon which a miracle is founded, may possibly amount to a entire proof...But it is easy to shew, that we have been a great deal too liberal in our concession, and that there never was a miraculous event established on so full an evidence.[66]

As an historian, Hume was concerned to establish criteria which could be used in assessing documentary evidence of past events. David Fate Norton addresses several of these criteria that Hume applied when considering such documents.[67] With regard to reports of "miracles," Hume's criteria are given in Part II of "Of Miracles."[68] The requirements for acceptance of testimony to a miracle by the "wise man" are very stringent. This is as it should be, however, since the claim that a miraculous resurrection occurred has such profound implications.

Hume initially states the "circumstances...requisite to give us a full assurance in the testimony of men."[69] First, the testimony must be given by "a sufficient number of men, of such unquestioned good-sense education and learning, as to assure us against all delusion in themselves."[70] This is a very strong requirement but, as Gaskin points out, "Hume's background was a theology which took the Gospels as straightforward factual reports. Against *that* background 'these criteria' would be quite in order."[71] I shall argue that they are in order for assessing testimony, especially testimony of such moment. Second, the testimony must be given by people of "undoubted integrity" so that we may be confident that there is no intention to deceive others.[72] If there were good reason to believe that there was an intention to deceive, the testimony would be undermined.

The first criterion Hume gives speaks to a person's competence in making a sound judgement. The second relates to the motivations of the people giving the testimony.[73] A good reason to believe that testimony was not given with the intention to deceive is that those giving it have,

> such credit and reputation in the eyes of mankind, as to have a great deal to lose in case of their being detected in any falsehood; and at the same time, attesting facts performed in such a public manner and in so celebrated a part of the world, as to render the detection unavoidable.[74]

These criteria are quite strong, and as Gaskin says,

> In the light of modern scholarship it might seem absurd to expect the Biblical narrative to satisfy such requirements and it should come as no surprise to *us* when Hume implies that the biblical narratives do not satisfy the requirements.[75]

They are strong requirements, but they are neither question-begging nor inappropriately severe in the circumstances.

A third criterion Hume lays down is what might be called the criterion of "antecedent probability." This is how he states it: "what we have found to be the most usual is always the most probable,"[76] i.e., we ought to judge the likelihood of an event to be the more improbable the more unusual the reported event is claimed to be. This third criterion is not directly related to the character of the "witnesses," but rather to the kind of event being testified to. There is another consideration of this kind. It is that reports of miracles "chiefly abound" among "ignorant and barbarous" peoples, with the related point that such reports are found in "the first histories of all nations."[77]

Now, if we limit our consideration of these criteria to the reports that Hume seems mainly concerned with, i.e., the Resurrection, then we can say Hume gives "tough-minded"[78] requirements that are not question-begging and which are appropriate to what is being claimed. They are not question-begging because Hume nowhere assumes, in simply giving these criteria, that the reports of the Resurrection are false. They are appropriately tough-minded because the whole meaning and conduct of one's life would be significantly altered were one to come to believe the reports where one had not previously been a "believer" and this is not a change that should be undertaken on the basis of anything less than very strong reasons indeed. Acceptance may lead one to beatitude or to the unnecessary fears and anxieties associated with superstition.

Hume's criteria for accepting testimony to the occurrence of a miracle come to this:

1) We must have reason to think that the people giving the testimony are sincere; their motivation in giving it is simply to tell the truth. A good reason could be that they have "credit and reputation" and a good deal to lose if "detected in any falsehood."

2) We must have reasons to think that the people giving the testimony are competent to make a judgement concerning the truth of what they report. If we knew they were educated and of "good-sense," then this would lend support to their testimony. If we had reason to believe the opposite, then the testimony would be undermined.

3) We must consider the circumstances under which that to which they are testifying is supposed to have taken place. Are the circumstances such that the event testified to took place in a "public manner" and in a "celebrated part of the world?" If the answer is yes, then this lends support to the testimony. If the answer is no, then the testimony is undermined; all other things being equal, the testimony would be helped or hurt by the circumstances under which the event was supposed to have taken place.

4) We must consider the antecedent probability of the event. The more extraordinary the event testified to, the less assured we can be that it occurred; "what we have found to be the most usual is always the most probable."

These criteria are all informal. That is, an event may have taken place even though the testimony to its occurrence failed to meet any of Hume's criteria. But they are in practice quite useful and they can be applied in a responsible way to historical documents as well as to other cases of testimony.

Suppose a good friend of yours, an astronomer friend, told you during the course of a serious conversation about "the heavens," that a total eclipse of the moon took place, visible over the west coast of the United States, while you slept at 3 o'clock last Saturday morning. According to Hume's criteria you would have very good reasons for believing her. While the event still might not have taken place, you could be pretty well assured in your judgement that it had.

Since the testimony to the eclipse was given during the course of a serious conversation with a good friend, there would be no reason not to think it was sincerely given. And in any case you could easily detect her in the falsehood. Her "credit and reputation" with you would be hurt if you did detect a falsehood, so she would have something to lose by lying. She would have a good deal to lose, if her friendship with you was very important, since insincerity between friends undermines a friendship. Hume's first criterion is met.

You might not believe your friend merely on the basis of the fact, as you believe, that the testimony was sincerely given. Does she know what she is talking about? Is she competent in this area? She is educated and interested in the field related to the testimony she has given. Hume's second criterion is met.

The event testified to by your friend is/was a publicly observable event. It is said to have taken place in a "celebrated part of the world." This would make it fairly easy to find corroboration or disconfirmation. The public manner of the event and the area of the world in which it is said to have taken place make it that Hume's third criterion is met.

How likely is it that such an event could take place? Is the event very unusual? Is it extraordinary? A total lunar eclipse is unusual enough to be interesting. But it is not very unusual and it is not statistically extraordinary. So, Hume's fourth criterion is met and you have very good reasons for accepting the testimony as true.

If we apply these informal and useful criteria to the testimony regarding the resurrection in the New Testament writings, then the difficulties which must be overcome in order to judge the testimony to be credible are greatly increased.[79] The consensus among current biblical scholars is that the New Testament writings are themselves "second-hand" recordings of reports. Collectively, they were written some fifteen to seventy years after the events testified to. They were written in Greek, so that it is very unlikely that they could have been written by the fishermen who followed Jesus and to whom, it is said, he appeared after he had risen. And we are not in possession of the original writings.

There are indications in the New Testament that the original followers of Jesus were themselves illiterate, but even waiving this possibility, they would have had to have been bilingual and literate in two languages, Greek and Aramaic, in order to have written the reports themselves. This is possible, but unlikely. It is more likely that an oral tradition existed which the earliest Resurrection accounts drew upon.

Even if they were sincere, they could have been credulous. Let us grant that they were sincere. There is evidence in the New Testament to the effect that Jesus' followers were dejected and disillusioned after his death. The "Jesus movement" was in a state of confusion when Jesus is reported to have reappeared alive and well with all the wounds received during his crucifixion still in evidence. It is possible that a desire to be relieved of their dreary states of mind led to self-deception without any intention to deceive others, but such a desire could foster credulity.

The Resurrection is not claimed to have taken place in a public manner. In fact, *no one reports actually having observed it*. What is testified to is that Jesus appeared after he had been resurrected. When he "appeared," it was to his own followers. The New Testament does include a report by a follower, or a follower of a follower, that Jesus appeared to five hundred others before he "ascended" into heaven. This is perhaps a later interpolation. We do not have the testimony of these five hundred reported witnesses, who can have no "credit and reputation" with us simply because they are unknown. We can only accord the follower "credit and reputation" by the New Testament literature itself and the context of the era as scholarly investigations reveal it to us. I need not go on with this synopsis at great length, since the results of contemporary scholarship are well known and available for anyone's perusal.

The case of the testimony of the "astronomer friend" is intended to show that Hume's criteria for assessing testimony are fair and reasonable. No questions are begged by the criteria against the occurrence of the Resurrection. But an application of fair and reasonable criteria to the New Testament reports of the Resurrection does undermine the credibility of the reports. Hume says,

> Our most holy religion is founded on Faith, not on reason; and it is a sure method of exposing it to put it to such a trial as it is, by no means, fitted to endure. To make this more evident, let us examine those miracles, related in scripture...[80]

He then assumes the criteria laid out earlier, considers the Pentateuch and its authors, and declares,

> I desire anyone to lay his hand upon his heart, and after a serious consideration declare, whether he thinks that the falsehood of such a book, supported by such a testimony, would be more extraordinary and miraculous than all the miracles it relates; which is, however, necessary to make it be received, according to the measures of probability above established.[81]

Christianity is a religion which has at its core a sacred literary tradition. This sacred literature contains testimony to the occurrence of miracles. The miracles reported in this literary tradition are taken to be the instituting and validating or justifying phenomena of "Christian Doctrine." But David Hume provides very good reasons to believe "that no human testimony can have such force as to prove a miracle, and make it a just foundation for any such system of religion."[82]

Hume's Implausibility argument proceeds by way of an assessment of testimony to the occurrence of a miracle; the Resurrection is the miracle of chief concern. Its conclusion is that it is implausible to believe that the Resurrection occurred, based solely on the testimony offered in its support. I believe it is successful and that it is successful for even stronger reasons when we add to it the successful conclusion of the Indistinguishability argument. The conclusion of that argument is that we could not distinguish a miracle from an anomaly, since strong evidence that a miracle did in fact occur would make it a reasonable question whether we had understood the laws of nature sufficiently, i.e., it would make it reasonable to wonder whether there was a violation of a law or whether there was no law which could have been violated to begin with. This conclusion makes the Implausibility of the testimony to the occurrence of a miracle even stronger because it puts into question the competence of those giving the testimony to make a sound judgement as to whether the event was miraculous or merely a presently unexplainable natural event. Lack of competence on the part of the "witnesses" to make a sound judgement concerning that to which they are testifying undermines the credibility of the reports.

Hume's conviction that we live in a shared cosmos is presupposed throughout the entire essay, "Of Miracles." That there are laws of nature which give rise to constant conjunctions between events is a basic assumption underlying both the Impossibility argument and the Indistinguishability argument. The Impossibility argument only succeeds if the miracle-claimer shares this assumption. But both Hume's own contemporaries and ours seem to share this assumption when they argue that a miracle is indeed a supernatural "suspension" of "the ordinary course of nature." Once this assumption is given up, the Impossibility argument has no purchase. But the Indistinguishability argument is formidable whether the "believer" believes that we live in a deterministic universe or an indeterministic one.

Hume's intention in "Of Miracles" to undermine belief in miracles is instrumental to a more far-reaching goal. All religion "except the philosophical and rational kind" becomes "a cover to faction and ambition."[83] The immanentist principles of "genuine" religion, the "religious" naturalism of Hume himself, serve in their "proper office," which is to "regulate the heart of men," and to enforce the "motives of morality and justice."[84] Hume had argued that we could not know that there was a necessary connection between "objects," but, as John Laird has observed,

> Nevertheless, and rather unexpectedly it would appear that Hume accepted the general uniformity of nature in the same unreserved (although ultimately alogical) sense as he accepted causal uniformities. This is plain...from his *attitude* to alleged exceptions, particularly 'miracles'...[85]

Hume's opposing of his own religious naturalism to the supernaturalism of Christianity is motivated by an overriding ethical concern. In the *Enquiry* Hume says that we must "cultivate true metaphysics with some care, in order to destroy the false and adulterate," "Happy, if we can unite the boundaries of different species of philosophy, by reconciling profound enquiry with clearness, and truth with novelty! And *still more happy*, if, reasoning in this easy manner, we can undermine the foundations of an abstruse philosophy, which seems to have hitherto served only as a shelter to superstition, and a cover to absurdity and error!"[86] His ultimate goal in carrying on the war against "superstition" into "the most secret recesses of the enemy" is to replace the supernaturalism of Christianity with an immanentist position which takes a shared cosmos to be the ultimate reality and thereby clears the path to the greater happiness of humanity.

# Chapter IV

## Notes

1. David Hume, *Enquiries Concerning Human Understanding and Concerning the Principles of Morals*, ed. L.A. Selby-Bigge (Oxford: Oxford University Press, 1980), p. 110.
2. David Hume, "Of Superstition and Enthusiasm," *David Hume: Writings on Religion*, ed. Antony Flew (La Salle, Illinois: Open Court Publishing, 1992), p. 5.
3. Ibid., p. 3. In the opening line of his essay, "Of Superstition and Enthusiasm," Hume says, "*That the corruption of the best things produces the worst,* is grown into a maxim, and is commonly proved, among other instances, by the pernicious effects

of *superstition* and *enthusiasm*, the corruptions of true religion." Hume's own "true religion," religious naturalism, sees the "cosmos" itself as the Eternal reality.

4. Hume, *Enquiry*, pp. 6–7 and p. 16.
5. Ibid., p. 127.
6. The Epistle of Paul to the Romans: 4:23–25; 5:1.
7. Benjamin F. Armstrong argues that Hume is guilty of question-begging in his essay, "Hume on Miracles: Begging Questions Against Believers," *History of Philosophy Quarterly* 9 no. 3 (July 1992). J.C.A. Gaskin maintains that, "Hume's contention at the beginning of Part II, that the evidence for a miracle has never amounted to a full proof, if not capable of justification for *all* cases, is at least justified when applied to the miracles which really matter; the biblical miracles in general and the Resurrection miracle in particular." *Hume's Philosophy of Religion* (Atlantic Highlands, New Jersey: Humanities Press Int., 1988), p. 158. I will discuss Hume's faith and how he opposes it to supernaturalist faith in the course of the present chapter. Clear statements of this cosmic faith, or religious naturalism, can be found throughout Hume's writings. An example can be offered from the *Natural History of Religion*, which is also set in a context of the fight against superstition. In Sect. II of the *Natural History*, Hume says, "All things in the universe are evidently of a piece. Everything is adjusted to everything. One design prevails throughout the whole," Root edition, p. 26.
8. Hume, *Enquiry*, p. 131. It may be thought to be an unintended irony of the essay "Of Miracles," that its' last sentence, in which Hume talks about faith undermining rationality, can be applied with little modification to Hume's own "religious naturalism." Since it may be said that Hume cannot consistently believe in the presence of a shared cosmos, his faith can be seen to undermine or "subvert all the (skeptical) principles of his understanding." He cannot consistently believe in a shared cosmos because the three basic components of this belief, self, objects or an objective world, and causality, Hume's "natural beliefs," have no corresponding impressions (except for causality or necessary connection, but this is a projected impression of reflection, not an impression of sensation). And Hume defines "belief" as a "...lively idea related to or associated with a present impression" in *A Treatise of Human Nature*, ed. L.A. Selby-Bigge and P.H. Nidditch (Oxford: Oxford University Press, 1980), p. 96. Both faith and doubt are elements of religious naturalism. His doubt is expressed in his epistemology and his faith is expressed in his "natural beliefs." "My practice, you say, refutes my doubts...As an agent, I am quite satisfied in the point." *Enquiry*, p. 38. He should have been quite satisfied indeed, since this in brief is his own objection to "excessive skepticism," *Enquiry*, pp. 158–159.
9. I am indebted to Rae Reich for isolating the terms of identification applied to Hume's arguments: Impossibility, Improbability, Implausibility and Indistinguishability.
10. Antony Flew, *David Hume: Of Miracles* (La Salle, Illinois: Open Court, 1990), pp. 3–12. This is a separate edition of Hume's essay, with notes and commentary by Anthony Flew. Armstrong criticizes what he refers to as the "Flew/Mackie response to the 'begging-the-question' charge," pointing out that this charge goes back to George Campbell's 1763 *Dissertation on Miracles*. Armstrong,

"Hume on Miracles: Begging-The-Question Against Believers," p. 319.

11. Insofar as Hume discusses the relevance of historical testimony in attempting to establish the occurrence of a miracle, I will endeavor to apply some insights which I have derived from Larry Wright's treatment of "testimony arguments" in his *Practical Reasoning*. Larry Wright, *Practical Reasoning* (San Diego: Harcourt, Brace, Javonovich, 1989) pp. 166–175.

12. Hume, *Enquiry*, pp. 109–110.

13. Flew, *David Hume: Of Miracles*, p. 56n1.

14. Tillotson's argument is quoted by David Fate Norton in his *David Hume: Common Sense Moralist, Skeptical Metaphysician* (Princeton: Princeton University Press, 1982), p. 297, from Tillotson's "A Discourse upon Transubstantiation" in *The Works of John Tillotson*, London, (1714).

15. Ibid.

16. Ibid.

17. Ibid.

18. Ibid. Actually, it is not clear that Tillotson's argument is relevant to Transubstantiation, since that theological doctrine allows that the sensory appearance of the host remains the same, despite substantial transformation. It is clear, though, that the purported New Testament miracles are held by Tillotson to rest on the evidence of sensory experience as reported by "eyewitnesses." Flew believes that Tillotson's understanding of Transubstantiation, "...suggests a remarkable lack of theological sophistication." Flew, op. cit., p. 56. But, rather than being seen as laboring under a misunderstanding of Catholic doctrine, Tillotson's argument might also be seen as offering a corrective to it from the Anglican point of view, just as Hume's argument would, "if just," convince the "wise and learned."

19. Hume, *Enquiry*, p. 109. Ironically, the "operation of the Holy Spirit" would itself be miraculous.

20. Tillotson, quoted by Norton, op. cit., p. 297.

21. Hume, *Enquiry*, p. 109.

22. Ibid., p. 110.

23. Ibid.

24. Ibid.

25. Ibid.

26. Ibid.

27. Ibid.

28. Ibid.

29. Ibid., p. 111. It seems plausible to take "experiments" to be roughly synonymous with "experiences" or observations.

30. Ibid.

31. Ibid.

32. Ibid.

33. Ibid.

34. Ibid.

35. Ibid., p. 113.

36. Ibid., p. 112–113.

37. Ibid., p. 114.
38. Ibid., p. 115.
39. Norton, op. cit., p. 298.
40. Hume, *Enquiry*, p. 114. Emphasis added.
41. Ibid., p. 114–115. Emphasis added. For the present purposes, it does not matter whether the requirement of necessary and sufficient conditions being stated for constant conjunctions is inadequate as a criterion for the statement of a "law of nature." I do not attribute this to Norton. What I think is important is the fact that Hume distinguishes constant conjunctions from laws.
42. Ibid., p. 115.
43. Ibid., p. 54. This is also affirmed on p. 30 and in the *Treatise*, ed. Selby-Bigge, Part XXII.
44. Hume, *Dialogues*, p. 94. Aiken edition. The Philonic Proposition.
45. Hume, *Enquiry*, p. 115.
46. Ibid.
47. Hume, *Enquiry*, p. 114. Emphasis added.
48. Antony Flew, quoted by Armstrong in "Hume on Miracles," p. 320: Antony Flew, "The Impossibility of the Miraculous," *Hume's Philosophy of Religion: The Sixth James Montgomery Hester Seminar* (Winston-Salem: Wake Forest University Press, 1986), p. 10.
49. Hume, *Enquiry*, p. 115.
50. Armstrong, "Hume on Miracles," p. 320.
51. Not all commentators refer to a single argument. Norton thinks "Hume's attack on miracles...is twofold." David Fate Norton, *David Hume: Common Sense Moralist, Skeptical Metaphysical*, p. 296. Flew distinguishes between, "What he (Hume) is trying to demonstrate a priori in Part I...", and the argumentation in Part II of the essay "Of Miracles." Antony Flew, "Fogelin on Hume on Miracles." *Hume Studies* 16 no. 2, (November, 1990): pp. 141–144. But Passmore refers to "*the* argument of that chapter," when referring to "Of Miracles." John Passmore, *Hume's Intentions* (London: Cambridge University Press, 1980), p. 32. Emphasis added. More judiciously, however, Passmore refers to "Hume's *discussion of miracles*" on p. 171. It is not unusual to distinguish Part I and Part II as containing different argumentation. Keith Yandell, for example, distinguishes between Part I and "Hume's Subsidiary Arguments" in Part II. Keith Yandell, *Hume's "Inexplicable Mystery"* (Philadelphia: Temple University Press, 1990), pp. 315–338. J.C.A. Gaskin also distinguishes several arguments. J.C.A. Gaskin, *Hume's Philosophy of Religion*, pp. 135–165.
52. Armstrong, "Hume on Miracles," p. 319. The only argument that would "rule out" miracles is the Impossibility argument.
53. Ibid., p. 321.
54. Ibid.
55. Again, it seems to be what I have called the Impossibility argument that Armstrong has in mind here. Other considerations seem to reinforce this view. If the believer were convinced that miracles are improbable, or that testimony regarding a miracle was implausible, or that we couldn't distinguish miracles from anomalies, the

believer could still go on believing. But if the believer were persuaded that miracles are impossible, then he would cease to be a believer in miracles. They would be "ruled out." The Impossibility argument only "rules out" calling events miraculous in the traditional sense of the term "miracle."

56. Armstrong, "Hume On Miracles," p. 321. Gaskin seems correct in saying that the miracles which "really matter" are the Biblical "miracles" and particularly the Resurrection, i.e., these are the ones that really matter to people in the Judeo-Christian tradition, with the Resurrection really mattering to the Christians in that tradition. And it mattered to Hume to undermine belief in these "miracles."

57. Hume, *Enquiry*, p. 128.

58. Armstrong, "Hume On Miracles," p. 322.

59. Ibid., p. 321.

60. Tillotson, quoted by Norton, *David Hume*, p. 297.

61. Armstrong, "Hume On Miracles," p. 322.

62. The letter is quoted by Norton and Popkin in their *David Hume: Philosophical Historian* (Indiana: Bobbs-Merrill Co., Inc., 1965), pp. 402–404.

63. Hume's view that the universe is a cosmos seems to be endorsed by the empirical science of his time. But for a contemporary empiricist, as Alexander Rosenberg points out, "It is unreasonable to deny that the world is basically and inexplicably indeterministic." It is "unreasonable" because the "message" of contemporary physics is that, "At the most fundamental level the local matters of particular fact that constitute the history of our world instantiate no exceptionless universal nomological generalizations...Accordingly, no two events in the actual world bear the relation of *Humean* causation to one another." Alexander Rosenberg, "Causation, Probability And The Monarchy," *American Philosophical Quarterly* 29 no. 4 (October, 1992): p. 305. "Heisenberg had discovered the uncertainty principle, and Bohr had discovered the principle of complementarity. Together these two principles constituted what became known as the 'Copenhagen interpretation' of quantum mechanics—an interpretation that convinced most physicists of the correctness of the new quantum theory. The Copenhagen interpretation magnificently revealed the internal consistency of quantum theory, a consistency which was purchased at the price of renouncing the determinism...of the natural world." Heinz Pogels, "Uncertainty and Complementarity," *The World Treasury of Physics, Astronomy, And Mathematics,* ed. Timothy Ferris (Boston: Little, Brown and Co., 1991), p. 97.

64. Thomas Aquinas, *Summa Contra Gentiles*, III, 100, quoted by Antony Flew. "Miracles," *Encyclopedia of Philosophy*, vol. 5, ed. Paul Edwards (New York: Macmillan Publishing Co., 1967), p. 346.

65. Armstrong, "Hume on Miracles," p. 322. The parenthetical remark is in the text. It is clear from this passage that Armstrong does not want to give up the traditional notion of a "miracle," so that an "act of God" does turn out to be a "miracle," a violation of a law of nature which has God as its cause.

66. Hume, *Enquiry*, p. 116.

67. David Fate Norton, "History And Philosophy In Hume's Thought;" Norton and Popkin, *David Hume: Philosophical Historian*, p. xlii.

68. My account of Hume's criteria is influenced by J.C.A. Gaskin in his *Hume's Philosophy of Religion,* pp. 155–159, and by Larry Wright's discussion of "testimony arguments" in his *Practical Reasoning,* pp. 166–175.

69. Hume, *Enquiry,* p. 117.

70. Ibid., p. 116.

71. Gaskin, *Hume's Philosophy of Religion,* p. 156.

72. Hume, *Enquiry,* p. 117.

73. "The standard way to undermine testimony—to attack its value as evidence—is to explain it away. We show it to be motivated not by its truth but by a wish to deceive, for instance, or, perhaps, to stem from incompetence or error." Larry Wright, *Practical Reasoning,* p. 169. In Chapter 4 of *Practical Reasoning,* Larry Wright includes a discussion of "testimony arguments."

74. Hume, *Enquiry,* pp. 116–117.

75. Gaskin, *Hume's Philosophy of Religion,* p. 156. We can assure ourselves that these requirements are not met by the biblical narratives by reading the article, "Biblical Literature" in the *Encyclopedia Britannica* Macropedia, 15th ed. vol. 2, (Chicago: Encyclopedia Britannica Inc., 1978), pp. 879–977.

76. Hume, *Enquiry,* p. 117.

77. Ibid., p. 119.

78. This is Gaskin's term in *Hume's Philosophy of Religion,* p. 156.

79. What follows is a brief synopsis of current thinking based on several sources. These are the article "Biblical Literature" in the Encyclopedia Britannica, 15th ed. vol. 2; Howard Clark Kee's *Jesus in History: An Approach to the Study of the Gospels,* second ed. (San Diego: Harcourt Brace Jovanovich, 1977); Thomas Sheehan's *The First Coming; How the Kingdom of God Became Christianity* (New York: Random House, 1986). Thomas Sheehan is professor of philosophy at Loyola University, Chicago. Part II of his book includes a very interesting discussion of how the belief in the resurrection of Jesus evolved, as Sheehan reconstructs the history.

80. Hume, *Enquiry,* p. 130.

81. Ibid.

82. Ibid., p. 127.

83. Hume, *Dialogues,* p. 88. Aiken Edition.

84. Ibid.

85. John Laird, Hume's *Philosophy of Human Nature* (London: Methuen & Co., Ltd., 1982), p. 107. Hume's writings on religion provide a context in which this "attitude" can be understood as an expression of Hume's own religious faith.

86. Hume, *Enquiry,* p. 12, p. 16 (emphasis added).

# Summary and Conclusions

In the preceding chapters I have developed a view of Hume's philosophical stance which I call "religious naturalism." This is a complex of metaphysical, epistemological, and ethical elements in which the universe is seen as a shared cosmos. The complex idea of a shared cosmos is comprised of Hume's three "strong natural beliefs," which are the belief in the existence of an *objective world*, in persons or *selves* who inhabit the world, and in *necessary causal* relations among and between selves and the rest of the objective world. My view of Hume highlights his aesthetic response to the "design" of the universe. This is to be distinguished from belief in an "intelligent designer of the universe." For Hume, the cosmos itself is the eternal reality.

Among the regularities of nature for Hume is the fact that our own human nature necessitates our believing in nature-at-large. As reflective beings, as thinkers in our studies we can suspend belief in the existence of nature. But not as active agents. To act effectively in the world we must believe it exists and that there are causal relations such that we can make plans and achieve goals and accomplish our purposes. As thinkers we may be skeptics, but as actors, never. There is a tension here analogous to a religious tension between faith and doubt.

In assessing Hume's philosophy of religion, the approach taken here is one of examining Hume's treatment of several topics which could come under the heading of traditional religious beliefs and then bringing the results to bear on an interpretation of Hume's overall philosophical stance. These beliefs include a belief in a deity of a certain nature, and belief in miracles. The first questions I address are; whether, in what way, and to what extent, if any, Hume thought religious beliefs to be "natural." I argue in support of Tweyman's criteria for Hume's "natural beliefs." I also argue that Tweyman's list of criteria needs supplementation and that the criteria, taken together, do not apply to a belief in an "intelligent designer of the universe" and so such a belief is not a "strong natural belief" for Hume.

I argue that Hume held a "naturalistic" as opposed to a "supernaturalistic" view of the world, but that the appropriate way to think of this naturalism is as a complex of metaphysical, epistemological and ethical concerns and views, viz., "religious naturalism." I call this naturalism "religious" because it encompasses both faith and doubt in certain metaphysical truths which are related to overriding ethical concerns.

As a firm conviction in a metaphysical view which cannot be proven, this naturalism itself bespeaks an element of faith. It is a faith in the "givenness" of a shared world ordered by natural laws which are "secret" and "inexplicable." Hume believed, moreover, that the adoption of this view could further the happiness of humanity. This motivates his war against "superstition." Hume's praise of True Religion and his Metaphysical Naturalism can both receive their due in a view of Hume's position that highlights the tension between metaphysical faith and epistemological doubt and relates this to Hume's ethical concern, which is to promote the happiness of persons.

Humean reflections on religious questions are contained throughout the corpus of his work. His *Natural History of Religion* is specifically devoted to understanding historical religious traditions as resulting from certain propensities of human nature. That humans share a common set of propensities is part of Hume's metaphysical faith.

Some Humean "propensities" are such as result in natural beliefs, in a very strong sense of that term. They are universal, instinctual and cannot be successfully resisted for any sustained period, e.g., the belief in causal relations. Others are such as give rise to beliefs that are not based on what Hume calls "primary instincts of human nature," but rather they are based on "secondary principles," e.g., belief in anthropomorphic deities. They are less than absolutely universal and they are resistible. Philosophy is the antidote to many of them.

I develop the distinction between "strong" and "weak" Humean natural beliefs, based upon Hume's distinction between "primary instincts" and "secondary principles" of human nature. I also begin to develop the conception of Hume's "religious naturalism," initially by way of a brief consideration of various supernaturalist positions which may be thought open to Hume. I offer a view which gives scholars their due who believe that Hume treats religious beliefs as natural, and so believe that Hume himself held a supernaturalist position. I argue that my reading of the *Dialogues* does justice to this view and at the same time clarifies the *actual* metaphysical status of the religious position that Hume held, which I am calling "religious *naturalism*."

I differ with scholars like Tweyman, Pike and Harris on the question of Hume's thin supernaturalism. It is a robust naturalism that provides the metaphysical content of Hume's faith.

With regard to the *Dialogues Concerning Natural Religion*, much depends on whether the "cause or causes" of order cited in Part XII must be transcendent to nature, imposing order from without, or whether "the cause or causes of order" might also be immanent, generating order from within. Hume's metaphysical faith, I argue, was a faith in causal relations obtaining in an objective universe in which we participate. A part of his religious naturalism was the faith that the universe is a *cosmos*. This faith, which could be doubted in reflective moments, but never forsaken, is to be distinguished from a faith in a supernatural designer of the universe.

This understanding of Hume's position can accommodate his extolling of True Religion, while at the same time dispensing with the "inconveniences" of attributing a supernaturalist position to him. It can accommodate the former, in part, by recognizing the self-conscious element of faith in Hume's metaphysical view, and by attentively considering the expressions of wonder, mystery, and what appears to be a kind of religious and/or aesthetic emotion in the *Dialogues*, a sense of the sublimity of the eternal cosmos even in the midst of skeptical doubt. These expressions of wonder, mystery, etc., are consistent with other aspects of Hume's thought such as his skepticism, which can be seen as mitigated with regard to experience, but unmitigated with regard to what is, in principle, beyond all possible experience. Yet Hume believes the cosmos is eternal.

Mitigated skepticism is the flip side of Hume's naturalistic faith. Just as faith and doubt are partners on the supernaturalist's path, they are partners on the path of Hume's religious naturalism. His metaphysical faith in a shared world and his skeptical doubt with regard to that very postulate go hand in hand.

Hume understood his belief in "nature" to arise from the functioning within "himself" (his imagination, his consciousness, his subjective experience) of the very object of his belief. He thought that the workings of "nature" within oneself gave rise to one's belief in "nature's" objective operations.

It is Hume's epistemological position that the existence of an objective world of causal relations cannot be known. Once doubts arise concerning its existence, the experience of an agent who is active in the world can only mitigate, but never completely eradicate, them. Nevertheless, Hume's faith is such that he trusts in the object of his faith, "nature," more than he trusts in the deliverances of his reason.

Hume's "religious naturalism" is exemplified in his discussion of miracles in the *Enquiry*. There are several possible arguments that could be identified in the essay on miracles, each with the aim of undermining belief in miracles:

The Impossibility argument, identified as an a priori argument, is the argument against the possibility of miracles. It is based on the assumption of the metaphysical element of Hume's religious naturalism. It is only successful if the burden of proof is on a miracle-reporter who believes in a "common course of nature." Hume does beg-the-question against resurrections by relying on his own judgement of the physical possibilities involved.

Secondly, an argument against the plausibility of accepting testimony as evidence for the occurrence of a miracle is offered by Hume. Here Hume considers the value of documentary testimony as evidence from an historian's perspective. This informal argument is successful in accomplishing Hume's main goal in "Of Miracles," it undermines the credibility of the Biblical miracle-reporters.

Thirdly, when an argument against the probability of miracles is based on the claim that since the more unusual an event is, the less probable it is that the event occurred, reports of extraordinary events ought to be judged very improbable.

The fourth is an argument against the possibility of distinguishing miracles from anomalies. It is against the possibility, for any given extraordinary putatively miraculous phenomenon, that empirical evidence alone could verify the fact that it is a miracle, rather than merely an anomaly. This is a successful argument which leaves open the abstract possibility of actual miracles, but it renders them less harmful from a Humean anti-superstitious perspective, because it renders them less capable of functioning as the foundations of a religion. Hume's targets here are religions which appeal to literary traditions containing reports of miracles which are then taken to be those religion's instituting and justifying or validating phenomena. He specifically cites Christianity. This argument is cogent whether one is a "Humean" determinist or an indeterminist.

I have argued that Hume's own metaphysical preconceptions are unhesitatingly employed in his "Of Miracles" and that Hume intended to supplant supernaturalism with a position he thought to be conducive to the greater happiness of humanity. This position was Hume's own "religious naturalism."

Religious Naturalism is a complex of metaphysical, epistemological and axiological positions and concerns. The axiological elements are ethical and aesthetic. The aesthetic element is Hume's "insistent feeling of design," as J.C.A. Gaskin calls it. It is Hume's aesthetic response to "nature," as can be seen in the *Dialogues* and other works. The ethical element in Hume's religious naturalism gives rise to his overriding concern to oppose his naturalistic faith to supernaturalism for the purpose of furthering the happiness of humanity. The epistemological element casts doubt on and tempers metaphysical faith. The metaphysical element of Hume's "religious naturalism" was his faith in the inexplicable presence of an eternal cosmos.

# Bibliography

Armstrong, Benjamin F. "Hume on Miracles: Begging Questions Against Believers." *History of Philosophy Quarterly* 9, no. 3, (1992).

Coppleston, Frederick. *A History of Philosophy.* Vol. 5. New York: Image Books, 1985.

Einstein, Albert. *Ideas and Opinions by Albert Einstein.* Ed. Carl Seelig et al New York: Crown Publishers, 1954.

Flew, Antony. "Fogelin on Hume on Miracles." *Hume Studies* 16, no. 2 (1990). Ontario.

———."Miracles." *Encyclopedia of Philosophy.* Vol. 5. Ed. Paul Edwards. New York: Macmillan Publishing Co., 1967.

———. *Hume's Philosophy of Belief.* New York: Humanities Press, 1961.

———. *David Hume: Philosopher of Moral Science.* New York: Basil Blackwell Ltd., 1986.

———. *David Hume: Writings on Religion.* La Salle, Illinois: Open Court Publishing, 1992.

———. *David Hume: Of Miracles.* La Salle, Illinois: Open Court, 1990.

Gaskin, J.C.A. *Hume's Philosophy of Religion.* Atlantic Highlands, New Jersey: Humanities Press Int., 1988.

Harris, H.S. "The 'Naturalness' of Natural Religion." *Hume Studies* 12 no. 1 (1987). Ontario.

Hume, David. *A Treatise of Human Nature.* Ed. L.A. Selby-Bigge and P.H. Nidditch. Oxford: Oxford University Press, 1980.

———. *A Treatise of Human Nature.* Ed. Ernest Mossner. London: Penguin Books, 1969.

———. *Dialogues Concerning Natural Religion.* Ed. Henry D. Aiken. New York: Hafner Press, 1984.

———. *Dialogues Concerning Natural Religion and The Natural History of Religion.* Ed. J.C.A. Gaskin. Oxford: Oxford University Press, 1993.

———. *Dialogues Concerning Natural Religion.* Ed. Nelson Pike. Indianapolis, New York: Bobbs-Merrill Co., 1970.

---. *Dialogues Concerning Natural Religion*. Ed. Norman Kemp Smith. Indianapolis; Thomas Nelson and Sons Ltd., 1947.

---. *Enquiries Concerning Human Understanding and Concerning the Principles of Morals*. Ed. L.A. Selby-Bigge. Oxford: Oxford University Press, 1980.

---. *Essays Moral, Political and Literary*. Ed. Eugene F. Miller. Liberty Classic, Liberty Fund Inc., 1978, Revised.

---. *The Natural History of Religion*. Ed. H.E. Root. Stanford: Stanford University Press, 1956.

Hurlbutt, Robert H. *Hume, Newton and the Design Argument*. Lincoln: University of Nebraska Press, 1985.

---. "The Careless Skeptic: The Pamphilian Ironies In Hume's *Dialogues*." *Hume Studies* 14 no. 2 (1988). Ontario.

Indinopolous, Thomas. *The Erosion of Faith*. Chicago: Quadrangle Books, 1971.

Kee, Howard Clark. *Jesus in History: An Approach to the Study of the Gospels*. 2d ed. San Diego: Harcourt Brace Jovanovich, 1977.

Klever, Wim. "Hume Contra Spinoza?" *Hume Studies* 16 no. 2 (1990). Ontario.

Laird, John. *Hume's Philosophy of Human Nature*. London: Methuen & Co., Ltd., 1982.

Moses, Greg. "Hume's Playful Metaphysics." *Hume Studies* 18 no. 1 (1992). Ontario.

Nelson, John O. "The Role of Part XII in Hume's *Dialogues Concerning Natural Religion*." *Hume Studies* 14 no. 2 (1988). Ontario.

Neto, Jose R. Maia. "Hume and Pascal: Pyrrhonism vs. Nature."*Hume Studies* 17 no. 1 (1991). Ontario.

Norton, David Fate. *David Hume: Common Sense Moralist, Sceptical Metaphysician*. Princeton: Princeton University Press, 1982.

Norton, David Fate and Popkin, Richard. *David Hume: Philosophical Historian*. Indiana: Bobbs-Merrill Co., Inc., 1965.

Passmore, John. *Hume's Intentions*. London: Cambridge University Press, 1980.

Penelhum, Terence. "Hume's Skepticism and the *Dialogues*." *McGill Hume Studies*. Ed. David Fate Norton et al. San Diego: Austin Hill Press, 1979.

Pogels, Heinz. "Uncertainty and Complementarity." *The World Treasury of Physics, Astronomy, And Mathematics*. Ed. Timothy Ferris. Boston: Little, Brown and Co., 1991.

Prado, C.G. "Hume And The God-Hypothesis." *Hume Studies* 7 no. 2 (1981). Ontario.

Rosenberg, Alexander. "Causation, Probability And The Monarchy." *American Philosophical Quarterly* 29 no. 4 (1992). Pittsburgh.

Sheehan, Thomas. *The First Coming; How the Kingdom of God Became Christianity.* New York: Random House, 1986.

Smith, Norman Kemp. *The Philosophy of David Hume.* London: Macmillan and Co. Ltd., 1947.

Tweyman, Stanley. *Scepticism And Belief In Hume's Dialogues Concerning Natural Religion.* Dordrecht: Martinus Nyhoff Publishers, 1986.

Wadia, Pheroze. "Philo Confounded." *McGill Hume Studies.* San Diego: Austin Hill Press, 1979.

Williams, B.A.O. "Hume On Religion." *David Hume: A Symposium.* New York: Macmillan & Co., Ltd., 1963.

Wright, Larry. *Practical Reasoning.* San Diego: Harcourt, Brace, Javonovich, 1989.

Yandell, Keith. *Hume's "Inexplicable Mystery": His Views on Religion.* Philadelphia: Temple University Press, 1990.

# Index

Note: Some entries that appear throughout the book, such as David Hume and the names of his works, are not listed in the Index. Page numbers for definitions are in italics.

acts of God. *See* miracles, as acts of God
aesthetic response. *See* design, insistent feeling of, as aesthetic response
ambiguity/ambiguous, 32, 37, 43, 55, 63
analogy (remote) to human intelligence. *See* Philonic proposition
animals. *See* natural beliefs, criteria: shared by humans and animals
animistic, 38, 39
anomaly. *See* miracles, arguments against: indistinguishability from anomalies
anthropomorphic/anthropomorphism, 29, 30, 32, 38, 40-43, 65
  assumptions of, 29
Aristotle. *See* God/gods, Aristotelian
Armstrong, Benjamin F., 84-88, 90, 97n7
attenuated deism. *See* deism, attenuated.
awe, feeling of. *See* religious naturalism, aesthetic qualities. *See also* Einstein, awe feeling of (as religious naturalism)

Bacon, Francis, 47
Bayle's Dictionary, 54. *See also* deism

beliefs
  "lively ideas" (Hume), *97n74*
  impressions and ideas, *2*, 4-7, 14, 47
  natural. *See* natural beliefs
  propension to, 5, 7, 13, 30, 34, 39
Blair, Hugh, 88, 89

causality, 3, 6-8, 16, 18, 22-24, 25n22, 29, 42, 58, 64, 97n8
  causal inferences, 2, 59
  "worlds in the making," 11, 35
  causal relations, 37-39, 41, 48, 57-59, 64, 68
  impressions of, 6, 7, 30. *See also* constant conjunctions
cause and effect, 9, 39, 42, 78. *See also* constant conjunctions
cause or causes of order in the universe. *See* Philonic proposition
Christian, 14, 30-33, 48, 76, 77, 82, 87, 100n56
  "sound, believing Christian," 30-32
Cleanthes (character in *Dialogues*), 1-3, 10-14, 16, 17, 20, 30, 31, 34-37, 43, 54, 62, 71n47
  illustrative analogies:
    articulate voice, 10, 11, 35, 36
    vegetable library, 10, 12, 35, 36
  philosophical position, 1
  self-evidence of design, 35, 36

common course of nature, 80, 74, 81, 87-89
common life, 58, 59
constant conjunctions, 9, 19, 36, 39, 74, 77-82, 84, 89, 95. *See also* common course of nature; uniformities; natural law/law of nature
cosmic religious feeling. *See* religious naturalism, aesthetic qualities
cosmos, 53, 54, 58-64, 68, 69, 73-75, 78, 89, 95, 96. *See also* universe
custom-generated beliefs, 21, 22. *See also* natural beliefs
custom and habit, 6. *See also* constant conjunctions

deism, 33, 40, 42, 43, 48-55, 57, 65, 67
  attenuated, 49-52, 55-57, 61, 64. *See also* Gaskin, J.C.A.
  Bayle's Dictionary, 54
  vague universal, 65
deity/deities. *See* God/gods, deity/deities
demiurge. *See* Platonic, Platonic demiurge
design argument, 1-4, 13, 34-36, 45n22, 52, 57, 61, 66, 69n2. *See also* teleological argument
  conclusion of. *See* intelligent designer, as conclusion of design argument
  as deistic argument, 52-54, 133
  vs. existence of a designer, 36
design, "insistent feeling of," 57, 63, 67. *See also* design argument; religious naturalism
  as aesthetic response (beauty), 62, 63, 72n62
  in J.C.A. Gaskin's "attenuated deism," 57
determinism/deterministic, 89, 95

doubt, 32, 48, 58-60, 64, 68, 97n8
Einstein, Albert, 43, 63-65, 68, 69, 72n53. *See also* religious naturalism, religious naturalists
  awe, feeling of (as cosmic religious feeling), 41
  relation to "art and science," 44
  metaphor of "reason," (as religious naturalism), 63, 65
empirical/empiricism, 9, 20, 22, 43, 75, 77-79, 82, 83, 100n63
empirical inquiry (Newton), 43
matters of fact, 49, 77
probability, 42, 75, 77, 78, 89
  applied to testimony, 77-79, 82
epistemological/epistemology, 48, 59, 60, 63, 68, 97n8
eternal, 54, 61, 62, 65,
  eternal, the, 71n49, 96n3
ethics/ethical, 33, 48, 59, 96
  ethical concern, 96. *See also* religious naturalism
excessive skepticism. *See* Pyrrhonism
external world, 5-7, 16, 18, 19, 23, 25n8, 29. *See also* natural beliefs

faith, 22, 31, 48, 58-60, 62-65, 67-69, 69n2, 70n30, 73-75, 78, 94, 101n85
  in an external world, 22, 48, 57-60
  and natural religion, 62-65, 67-69, 73-75, 78, 94
feeling, aesthetic. *See* design, insistent feeling of; religious naturalism, aesthetic qualities
fideist, 70n30. *See also* faith
Flew, Antony, 25n14, 27n67, 74, 84, 97n10, 98n18, 99n51

Gaskin, J.C.A., 47, 49-58, 60, 62, 64, 67, 90, 91. *See also* attenuated deism

God/gods. *See also* anthropomorphism; intelligent designer; revelation; superstition
agnostic, 42, 43
Aristotelian, 54
atheism, 42, 51, 54, 65
deity/deities, 30-33, 40, 41, 52, 54, 64, 65
  immanent, 33, 40, 42, 53, 54, 56, 62, 63, 73
  transcendent, 31, 33, 42, 50, 52-56, 60, 61, 64, 67, 68, 70n30, 72n51
"God or Nature" (Spinoza), 65, 71n49
monotheism, 32, 40
pantheism, 33, 40-43
polytheism, 38-41, 53, 67
theism/theist/theistic, 1, 12, 30, 32, 41-43, 47, 48, 51, 53, 54, 63-66
Thomistic, 54
as transcendent cause/causes of order, 33, 50-52, 55
universe as. *See* Philo, philosophical position

habit and custom. *See* custom and habit
happiness, 49, 52, 96
Harris, H.S., 3, 37, 57
human experience, 52
human nature, 3, 18, 37, 38, 40, 41, 48, 52, 65
Hurlbutt, Robert H., 2, 3, 11-13, 24, 29, 30, 37, 38, 57
  "the reformulated (design) argument," 13

ideas, 2, 4-7, 9, 14, 15, 19, 38, 40, 47, 49, 55, 65. *See also* beliefs, as impressions and ideas
lively ideas, 4, 25n1, 97n74
immanent. *See also* God/gods, immanent

immanent (*continued*)
  "this-worldly," 48, 52, 64, 68
  immanent/monistic, 53
  immanent/pluralistic, 53
implausibility argument. *See* miracles, arguments against: implausibility
impossibility argument. *See* miracles, arguments against: impossibility
impressions, 2, 4-8, 12, 14, 18, 19, 30, 37, 39, 47, 55, 97n8. *See also* beliefs
improbability argument. *See* miracles, arguments against: improbability
indistinguishability argument. *See* miracles, arguments against: indistinguishability from anomalies
induction, 12, 27n67, 35, 72n53
  principles/rules of, 12, 27n67, 35
inexplicable. *See* mystery, "inexplicable (Hume's)
intelligence, remote analogy to human. *See* Philonic proposition
intelligent designer, 1-3, 13-16, 18, 19-22, 24, 29, 33-41. *See also* Philonic proposition
  belief in:
    as not instinctual, 15, 24, 29
    as not necessary for survival, 24, 29, 41
    as not shared by humans and animals, 24, 29
    as not universal, 14, 24, 29, 38, 39, 43
    as conclusion of design argument, 2, 3, 14, 21, 34-36
    as natural belief. *See* natural beliefs, intelligent designer as
ironic/irony, 2, 30-33, 42, 51, 56, 97n8
  Gaskin's caution against Hume's irony, 56

ironic/irony (*continued*)
  ironic interpretation, *Dialogues*, Part XII), 33

Jesus Christ, 73, 76, 82, 83, 87, 93, 94
Johnson, Samuel, 54
Judeo-Christian, 48

Laird, John, 96
laws of nature. *See* natural law/law of nature

metaphysical/metaphysics, 43, 48, 52, 59-64, 66-69, 70n21, 74, 76, 80, 81, 85, 96
  neo-Platonic metaphysics, 70n21
miracles, 33, 51, 70n18, 70n19, 73-77, 79-92, 94, 95
  as acts of God, 87, 88
  arguments against:
    implausibility, 75, 85, 95
    impossibility, 75, 79, 82-90, 95
    improbability, 75
    indistinguishability from anomalies, 75, 79, 82-84, 90, 95
  resurrection as example of, 73, 74, 77, 81-95
  as violation of natural law. *See* natural law/law of nature, violation of
monotheism. *See* God/gods, monotheism
moral evidence, 77. *See also* probability/probabilities
Moses, Greg, 58, 61, 62
Mossner, Ernest, 65
mystery, 41, 62, 63, 68, 80
  "inexplicable" (Hume's), 43, 48, 62, 69, 79

natural beauty, 62, 63
natural beliefs, 1-10, 13-24, 29, 33-35, 37-40, 42, 55, 57, 59, 63, 97n8

natural beliefs (*continued*)
  awareness accompanying, 4, 7, 9, 14, 31, 63
  criteria:
    shared by humans and animals, 21-24
    survival value, 13, 22, 57, 58, 64
    Tweyman's criteria for, 4
  custom-generated beliefs, 21, 22
  intelligent designer as, 1-3, 13-16, 18, 19-22, 24, 29, 33-41
  non-controversial cases, 4, 34, 39, 42, 57
    body/external world/objects, continued and independent existence of, 5, 7, 8, 10, 25n22
    causality, 3, 6-8, 16, 18, 22-24, 29, 42, 58, 64, 97n8. *See also* causality
    self/personal identity, 2-5, 8-13, 15, 23, 25n22, 35, 36, 38, 63, 65, 68, 97n8
  strong (primary instincts)/weak (secondary principles, 37, 38
natural causes, 83
natural cosmos, 64, 73
natural forces, 54
natural law/law of nature, 33, 43, 48, 62, 64, 69, 70n18, 74, 79-87, 89, 90, 95. *See also* constant conjunctions; uniformities
  violation of, 33, 79-82, 84, 85, 89, 90, 95. *See also* miracles, arguments against
natural philosophy, 65
  philosophers of, 74, 78
natural propension, 5, 13
natural religion, 1, 48,
natural theology, 29, 32, 55, 67
naturalism. *See* supernaturalism, vs. naturalism. *See also* religious naturalism

nature
  "common course of," 74, 80, 81, 87-89, 89
  as a commonplace belief in Hume's work, 56, 62
  as determining belief and instinct, 19. *See also* natural beliefs
  "God or Nature." *See* God/gods, "God or Nature"
  "Nature" vs. principles of skepticism, 9
neo-Platonic metaphysics, 70n21
Neto, Joseph R. Maia, 58
Newton, Isaac, 43
Newtonian, 12
Norton, David Fate, 79, 80, 90, 99n51

object/objects, 1, 2, 4, 6-9, 19, 78
  objective world, 2, 57-59, 64, 68, 97n8
order
  cause or causes of. *See* Philonic proposition, order, cause or causes of
  Hume's conviction of, 58
  order-generating structural dynamic, 53
orderly, 59, 62, 65, 69n2, 74, 80, 86

pantheism. *See* God/gods, pantheism
parsimony, 53-55, 60, 61, 67, 68
  principle of, 53
Passmore, John, 85
Penelhum, Terence, 65, 67
personal identity. *See* natural beliefs, non-controversial cases of, self/personal identity
Philo (character of *Dialogues*), 1-3, 10-14, 16, 17, 18, 20, 21, 29-37, 40, 42, 43, 53-56, 58, 60-63, 65-68, 70n23
  philosophical position, 1, 2, 58
Philonic proposition, 32, 52-57, 60, 61, 63-68, *70n23*, 99n44

Philonic proposition (*continued*)
  analogy (remote) to human intelligence, 32, 40, 43, 50, 52, 53, 55, 57, 62-64, 66-68, 81
  order, causes or causes of, 32, 33, 40, 43, 50-58, 62-65, 67, 81
  "plain philosophical assent" to, 52, 55, 66-68
physics, 43, 100n63
Pike, Nelson, 66, 67
Platonic, 51, 58
  Platonic demiurge, 58
Pogels, Heinz, 89
polytheism. *See* God/gods, polytheism
Popkin, Richard, 89, 90
Prado, C.G., 3
primary instincts. *See* natural beliefs, strong (primary instincts)/ weak (secondary principles)
probabilities/probability, 42, 57, 74, 75, 77, 78, 91, 92, 94, 100n63. *See also* empirical
proof, 12, 23, 69n2, 76, 78-80, 82-88, 90, 97n7
Pyrrhonism, 58, 59

question-begging charge against Hume, 74, 84-88, 91

"reason," metaphor of. *See* Einstein, metaphor of "reason"
religion
  Hume's sense of, 42
  Philo's concessions to, 1
  traditional religion, Hume's antidote to, 49
  true religion (Hume), 47, *48*, 63
  true religiosity (Einstein), 63
religious naturalism, v, vi, 62-65, 68, 71n49, 74, 78, 80, 96, 96n3
  aesthetic qualities:
    aesthetic response 63, 67
    cosmic religious feeling, 43, 62, 97n7

religious naturalism, aesthetic qualities (*continued*)
   Einstein's "feeling of awe," 41
   insistent feeling of design, 63
   sense of wonder, 41, 43, 68
   circularity of reasoning in, 59, 68
   religious naturalists: Einstein, Hume and Spinoza as, 43, 71n49
remote analogy to human intelligence. *See* Philonic proposition
resurrection. *See* miracles
revelation, 31-33, 43, 54, 55, 70n19
   "flying to" revealed truth, 2, 13, 30-32, 34
   as informing reason, 52
   source of, 31-33

secondary principles. *See* natural beliefs, strong(primary instincts)/ weak (secondary principles)
self, 5, 8, 9-13, 15, 23, 35, 36, 47, 58, 63, 65, 68, 74, 97n8. *See also* natural beliefs, non-controversial cases, self/personal identity
shared cosmos. *See* universe, as shared cosmos
Sheehan, Thomas, 93
skeptical doubt, 59, 64, 68
skepticism, 9, 12, 30, 31, 42, 57, 59-61, 63, 68, 97n8
   excessive. *See* Pyrrhonism
   mitigated skepticism, 48, 57, 59
Smith, Norman Kemp, 2, 3, 23, 25n22, 48
Spinoza, Baruch, 43, 65, 71n49
stoic, 58
sublime/sublimity, 41, 43, 47, 68
supernaturalism, 47, 48, 51, 55-57, 61, 64, 66, 69, 73, 75, 96
   infinite regression potential, 60
   vs. naturalism, 47
   vs. religious naturalism, 73, 74

superstition, 29, 30, 32, 33, 48, 49, 61, 73, 74, 92, 96
   anthropomorphic beliefs as, 29, 30, 32, 38, 40-43, 65. *See also* God/gods
   "war against," 61, 73, 96
survival value *See* natural beliefs, criteria: survival value

teleological argument, 2, 42, 49, 52, 67. *See also* design argument
testimony, 73-79, 82, 85, 86, 90-95
   "astronomer friend" analogy, 92, 94
   historical criteria (Hume), 90-95
   Wright's discussion of, 101n68, 101n73
theism. *See* God/gods, theism/ theist/theistic
Thomas Aquinas, Saint, 89
Thomistic, 54
Tillich, Paul, 71n37
Tillotson, 76, 77, 81-83, 87, 89
   doctrine of transubstantiation, 76, 77, 81-83
transcendent, 31, 33, 42, 50, 52-56, 60, 61, 64, 67, 68, 70n30, 72n51. *See also* God/gods
   "other-worldly," 48, 52, 53, 65
   transcendent/monistic, 53-55, 60, 61, 64, 67, 68, 70n30, 72n51
   transcendent/pluralistic, 53
transubstantiation. *See* Tillotson, doctrine of transubstantiation
Tweyman, Stanley, 2-10, 13-22, 24, 30, 34, 37-42, 47, 57
   analysis of Humean natural beliefs, 4-10. *See also* natural beliefs

uniformities, 29, 69n2, 74, 79-81, 89, 96. *See also* common course of nature; constant conjunctions

universality, 9, 15-20, 39
　interpretations of:
　　contingent (conditional)/strict,
　　　16-20
universe
　as God. *See* Philo, philosophical
　　position
　indeterministic, 89, 95
　as shared cosmos, 59, 60, 69, 74,
　　78, 95, 96, 97n7

Wadia, Pheroze, 3
Williams, B.A.O., 3
"worlds in the making." *See*
　causality, causal inferences
Wright, Larry. *See* testimony,
　Wright's discussion of

Yandell, Keith, 44n20, 47, 99n51